A Journey Shared

A Journey Shared

◆

Selected Thoughts on Life from Greg's Head from GregsHead.net

Greg Campbell

iUniverse, Inc.
New York Lincoln Shanghai

A Journey Shared
Selected Thoughts on Life from Greg's Head from GregsHead.net

iUniverse books may be ordered through booksellers or by contacting:

iUniverse
2021 Pine Lake Road, Suite 100
Lincoln, NE 68512
www.iuniverse.com
1-800-Authors (1-800-288-4677)

All Scripture quotes are from the **New Living Translation** unless otherwise stated. *New Living Translation*—Copyright © 1996 by Tyndale Charitable Trust. Tyndale House Publishers, Inc. Wheaton, IL 60819. *(NIV) New International Version*—Copyright © 1973, 1978, 1984 by International Bible Society. P.O. Box 62970, Colorado Springs, CO 80962. *(MSG) The Message*—Copyright © 1993, 1994, 1995, 1996, 2000, 2001, 2002 by Eugene H. Peterson. NavPress Publishing Group, P.O. Box 35001, Colorado Springs, CO 80935.

Other Books Referenced Include:
It's Not About Me by Max Lucado. Copyright © 2004 by Max Lucado. Published by Integrity Media, Inc., 5250 Virginia Way, Suite 110, Brentwood, TN 37027.
Dangerous Wonder by Mike Yaconelli. Copyright © 1998 by Mike Yaconelli. NavPress Publishing Group, P.O. Box 35001, Colorado Springs, CO 80935.
He Loves Me by Wayne Jacobsen. Copyright © 2000 by Lifestream Ministries. Published by Insight Publishing Group, 8801 South Yale, Suite 410, Tulsa, OK 74137. www.lifestream.org

ISBN: 0-595-34635-9

Printed in the United States of America

Contents

Section 3: What Is Sin?

SECTION 4: The LORD Gave and the LORD Has Taken Away

SECTION 5: Learning To Trust

Introduction

January 31st, 2005

Hi. My name is Greg. You have already seen my head, it's on the cover of this book. This book has been an adventure for me. A Journey, as the title suggests. Most of the material published herein was first posted (grammatical errors and all) on my blog page. It has had several homes, but has finally rested at ***www.GregsHead.net***.

I am a writer at heart. I always have been. From my earliest childhood memories, that is what I wanted to do! So, the advent of the blog page has been a wonderful thing for me—a simple, fast, and *free* place to write about anything and everything. And that certainly has been what you can find at that website. There is definitely a good reason to call the page "Random & Wandering Thoughts From Greg's Head".

But I began to hear from people. Some simple comments, "Hey, good blog!" But a few were more in-depth. Some people were really touched by my blogs. I have heard that several folks have used them as personal devotionals, or even devotionals for group meetings. That is so great! My primary purpose for writing these "blogs" is not really for the reader. It is, (read ***Audience***) but mostly it is a way for me to process The Journey.

As comments continued to come in, a few suggested that I should print the blog for those who can not access the internet. (Namely, my Grandparents!) I thought it was worth checking into, so I did. I found iUniverse.com. They are the publishers of this book. They offered a great way for me to make the blog page (in an edited, and compiled, and organized way) available without having to go through a publisher who would require printing 1000s of copies up front! I did not want to do that. This way, the book will be available through my website, and through iUniverse.com and at Amazon.com, Barnes & Noble and more! Sounds like a great deal!

I am excited to share these writings in this format. As I went through and corrected spellings, and grammar and punctuation, and added or repaired sentences a necessary—I also got to relive the journey. What a year it has been. Every day with God is an adventure, but you string a year or a year and a half of those together, and you have quite a Journey.

And the Journey was meant to be shared.

You may not agree with all of the things I say. I have a friend who doesn't agree with *most* of the things I say. But hopefully you will hear things from my Journey with our Father that will encourage you. That will ring true in you. That perhaps, you can share with someone else.

Thank you for purchasing this book. It certainly helps us when you do. I encourage you to purchase copies for people who may be strengthened by reading the life shared within. But money is not the goal with this book. If you can share my Journey with another, please do. Please visit the blog page. It is updated quite often. Please send a friend there.

The Journey is meant to be shared. So please do.

See you inside…

Greg Campbell

SECTION 1

How Great Is Our God

Awareness

February 5th, 2004

I was just talking with God this morning, and something struck me. He is totally aware of how I am feeling, what I am saying, what my worries and fears are, where I am at rest…everything. He is completely aware of me.

But it doesn't stop there. He is aware of you. He knows what you are doing right now, he knows how you are feeling, he even knows what you are thinking.

But it doesn't stop there. At the same time he knows you and me, he is completely aware of *everyone* else! Not only those here on earth, but those who are with him in paradise. (Luke 23:43)

The Bible tells us a bunch just how much God knows us. It says in Psalm 139 that he "knit us together in our mother's womb" (which is fairly intimate knowledge…and goes back pretty far in our lives. "God and I? We go *way* back! All the way back to the womb!") Also in verse 4 it says, "Before a word is on my tongue you know it completely, oh Lord." And in Isaiah 49:1 it says, "Before I was born the LORD called me; from my birth he has made mention of my name." And elsewhere it talks about God knowing our hearts, not just looking at the outside.

How can he know ALL of that about ALL of us?? What an amazing God.

Then, after I thought all of that in one very cool instant, I read my daily Bible reading, and topped that off with a couple Max Lucado chapters. He is a great writer. Very simple, but just great stuff. And you know what it was about today?

Go ahead, take a guess.

Really.

Got it? What's your guess?

RIGHT! About how Jesus knows us. He referred quite often to Hebrews 2, where it talks about Jesus being like us in every way. He experienced *everything* you or I have ever, or will ever experience. So, when we need help…or when we "don't"…He's been there.

That is a great thing to know. Often I try and think of someone I can talk to about something I am going through in life. Many times it will be my parents.

Other times it's a close friend. Often it is Jen. But, many times, I just can't find anyone who is going through *exactly* what I am going through.

But he has. He is aware. He's been there, done that.

How incredible is our God. That he could be all things to all people. Even me!

100% God, 100% Man

February 13th, 2004

To our minds, there are limits. For instance, 100%. Means 100 parts per 100. You can not have more. That's it. 100% is the maximum limit. End of story. So, when Jesus claims to be 100% Man (Hebrews 2:17), and at the same time 100% God (Colossians 1:19, 2:9)—well, we know that's impossible.

Now most of us, being the good little Christians that we are, say that we accept that on the surface. But when it comes down to it, we know that it is actually impossible, so we end up taking sides. If not on that issue, then on another mystery of God issue.

The issue of Calvinism vs. Arminianism came up at our membership class the other night. This church takes the Arminian stand. They say that God gave us all free-will to choose him, and that anyone can be saved. Scripture backs them up.

The Calvinist on the other hand says that God has predestined all who will be saved. That it is God who does the choosing and the saving. Scripture backs them up.

WHAT!? They can't both be right??? Well, God has given us free-will, that is why we are in the mess we are in. We constantly make bad choices for ourselves and those around us. And, its says to all who believe he will give the right to be called children of God. That means all. But, it also says in many places that God is sovereign, that God has predetermined salvation, that we are elected…all sorts of language like that. I lean more toward the Arminian side, but I think there's something bigger here.

Jesus is 100% man, 100% God. God is 100% Father, 100% Son & 100% Spirit. And, all at once, he's 100% one being. God's numbering system is not ours. God can predestine and choose us all he wants, and still make free-will work—and we don't have to be able to understand it.

That is the main place we get into trouble. When we start trying to figure out *how* God does stuff, and not just trusting that He does. That is where doctrinal divides occur between Christian brothers. That is where arguments arise…and divide.

So, next time you are tempted to ask—or especially to *argue about*—how God did, does or will do some specific thing just remember…

Jesus is 100% man and 100% God. Added together, that makes 100%.

God's Faithfulness

June 29th, 2004

This past weekend was the last weekend on staff for our children's pastor. Her name is Rachael. She came to work here about the same time that we did, freshly graduated from Indiana Wesleyan University (where my cousin was a women's softball star!!! Really! She broke all kinds of school records! She's awesome!). Anyway, Rachael has done a fantastic job with the children's ministry, but felt like God was calling her on to something else in life. Not because she didn't like where she was—quite the opposite—just because she heard him calling.

So, she announced her resignation, and that she was moving to California to attend a Bible college out there. This was even before she had been accepted! She still does not have a job or a place to live or a lot of things you might think you "need" to have before you embark on a journey of this magnitude. I very much admire her faith in this! Very cool!

So, this past weekend, Rach (that's what they call her) got to preach at all the services, and she basically just told her story about this "walk of faith" she's on, and how God is faithful through it. And when everything else changes, we can hold on to his UN-change-ness.

That's where I come in.

Good weekend…we were leading some great songs that helped bring home the faithfulness of God idea—and how we want to be faithful too. And all was well, until we lost Ian. Between the 2nd and 3rd services…here's the e-mail I sent to our worship team later that day…

We Lost Ian!

You know, I actually got to taste a bit of the faithfulness of God that Rachael was talking about today—and specifically how he is faithful whether life is grand or ripping apart at the seams. In between the services today, we went to find Ian and he was not where he was supposed to be. He had been sitting with Rachael, and another friend while we sang and was then to go over to his class. So I was quite surprised to find that he was not in the room when we went to pick him up, and one of the ladies helping out there today said she had not seen him. We checked the sign-in sheet...no Ian!!! OK. That was weird. So, I asked around, checked around, and I could not find him!!!! AHHHHH!!!

At this point, nothing mattered to me except finding my son. I was asking God to help and looking everywhere I could. I was not frantic, but I was really quite concerned.

So, it ended up that he was in fact in his class room, where he was supposed to be...just not signed in. And somehow hiding or invisible when I was there, even the people helping there had not seen him. But, all was well in the end...WE FOUND HIM!!! That was a great relief. But something hit me as we sang our first song in the next service. It was slightly jarring. We were singing, "All of my days I will sing of your greatness, all of my days I will speak of your grace..." and I was forced to admit that even if my son was somehow gone, God would still be faithful.

God's faithfulness is not dependent on my surroundings. Often, we call Him faithful when things are going well for us, and indeed, that is a way that we know his faithfulness. But Life does not always go as we want it to...yet God is faithful. He is there with us no matter what might be going on around us. That is a clearer picture of His faithfulness. And he reminded me of that today.

Praise Him

July 28th, 2004

We sang a song this past week at camp that I have sung many times before. As we sang, I was reminded of the depth within one of the lines. We sang, "With every breath I'm praising You."

Actually, many times I have sung that and felt a twinge of guilt as I do not praise Him with my every breath. With many I am doing quite the opposite. Speaking harsh words to my wife and children. Speaking bitter words about those who have wronged me. Speaking words that just needn't be spoken.

But the depth of the statement revealed to me just how stuck on myself I still am.

I keep thinking that it's about me—what I do, who I am, even what I don't do. But it's really not. It's really all who God has made me to be. The depth of that statement comes in the wonder of my creation, not in my own acts of praising.

Just the very fact that I exist is praise to Him. The wonder of me is a testament to His greatness. Not anything that I can stake a claim on, just the creation of the Creator.

With every breath, I'm praising Him.

That said, I will continue to point every bit of life God has given me toward Him and tell everyone along the way that Jesus has given me life beyond what I could imagine. And in that way, I will also attempt to actively praise him with every breath.

But I rest in the fact that even if I don't try—with every breath I am praising Him.

And that's awesome.

God Works All Things For Good

Aug 8th, 2004

We were supposed to record on Thursday night. We had scheduled a session to begin tracking the drum parts. Sometime around 5 or 6pm. I had been calling the studio engineer (a friend of ours) to verify that appointment, but to no avail.

Until, about 10am Thursday morning…

"We did?! Oh man!" Those were not the words that I wanted to hear…

So, with *many* calls and much frustration, we managed to schedule a session on Thursday and Friday with another friend, Jesse, who runs a studio somewhat nearby. He was the engineer for our **Come As You Are** project. That project sounded great, so we were very much looking forward to this last-minute replacement session.

That evening, Dave and I proceeded to Dansville, NY to track the drum parts at The Illuminata—our friend's new studio right on Main St there in town. When we arrive, we catch up and hang out a bit as we are setting up…and in the process, I think I saw how God had arranged "bad" to be good.

Jesse had experienced an emotionally and physically draining week. He was busy, and had also just received some news that was hard to swallow. And he told us that night that we were a big encouragement to him. Just simply being there, recording session out of the blue, getting to re-connect.

God works all things together for good for those who love him.

Jesse loves him. I love him. Dave loves him. I think all in all, as insignificant as a couple studio sessions are, God was at work for all of us. Turning a slightly bad situation (messed up scheduling) into a great connection of people that encouraged each of us.

And, the drums sound great!!!

So when things are frustrating you, just stop. Take a breath, and ask God to show you where He's working. You already know He is. You just need to see it.

And then take a look around and watch as He works all things together for good for those who love Him.

Consistency

Aug 10th, 2004

Have you ever made or eaten home-made vanilla ice cream? It's so great! And a vivid memory from my childhood. My grandma was famous (amongst her grandkids, at least) for her home-made ice cream. We would have it every time we'd visit! She'd get out the ice cream making bucket and the ice. Then she'd pour that little mixture in the ice cream container and start the thing a crankin'! (Now, by the time I was around, Grandma had the electric kind, not the hand crank. She was pretty hip…)

If you have not seen one of these puppies in action, it's quite a sight to behold! There is a larger outer bucket that holds all of the crushed ice you pack in around the smaller, metal container. The smaller container rests on a pivot point in the middle of the larger container, and the motor spins the smaller container around while a mixing blade stays stationary, mixing the ice cream concoction as the small container rotates. So after 10–15 minutes of gears grinding and metal scraping through ice, Grandma would pull the plug, and start dishing out the ice cream! We were all so excited to eat it we couldn't wait! (Well, at least I WAS!)

I would dip my spoon in and get a bite in my mouth as quickly as I could! And every time, without fail, the first thing I noticed was…

The consistency. Not really the flavor, though that too was unique. The consistency was different than your store-bought variety. It was softer, but not like soft-serve. It was smoother, but not as creamy as some over-processed varieties. It was just different. And that made it awesome!

Last Thursday afternoon we got to make our first home-made ice cream of the summer. Over the past summer or two, we have not had much luck in achieving the above referenced consistency. Mostly, we ate slightly thicker ice cream soup. But this time, I think we got it! The ice cream is creamy, not crystallized, and it was even pretty solid when it first came out of the bucket. SUCCESS!!

That started me thinking. Consistency is quite important in life. We want our food to be the way it should be in our mouths. The way it should feel. The right consistency.

And it doesn't just stop at food. We want our life to make sense. We want our daily routines to be consistent. Consistent with the day before, the week before, just pretty much on par. Life is easier with the right consistency.

But have you noticed? Life is not consistent.

I try occasionally to make sure that I have a consistent morning routine, hoping that perhaps that consistency will create some kind of harmony in my life for the rest of the day. Most often…it doesn't.

I try to pray consistently for friends and family going through tough situations where they really need help. That consistency not only helps me, but others too. I try, but I fail.

I try to be consistent in my attitudes in life. In how I take in my surroundings and how I dish out my in-takings. But again, I am just not getting the right consistency.

Every once in a while I get it right, like with my ice cream. And it's great. But really, life is not about *our* consistency.

"Jesus Christ is the same yesterday, today and forever." (Hebrews 13:8)

He is our consistency. We are not. Family is not. Our routine is not. Our friends are not. Our jobs are not. The weather is not. Our favorite football teams are not. (Especially the Bills…)

There is a reason he is referred to as a Rock. He is just the right consistency in the middle of a bunch of failed attempts at home-made ice cream.

I think today, I am going to keep my eyes open for His consistent-ness. And savor the rich, creamy, smooth, perfect consistency of his home-made ice cream.

God Came

Dec 31st, 2004

You have seen the title before. It is the title of our latest CD. Our Christmas CD. So, it has been marketed, e-mailed and e-mailed, posted on web pages, plastered on posters, and made its presence known in various retail locations across upstate NY and various other locales in the good ol' US of A.

But they are not just examples of catchy commercialism. Not simply marketing genius.

They aren't even really my ideas.

Yes, I wrote the song "God Came" way back in 1994. And yes, we recorded the CD this year, and it is *awesome!* (One more shameless plug there...)

But that's neither the beginning, nor the end of this wonderful story.

All month long, we presented the amazing truth of how God loved us so much that he decided to give up his role as King of the universe and be born as a baby, grow up and give his life for us. We should have died, but instead, our King gave his life. Incredible. Too amazing. Incomprehensible.

And it is. But, Paul prayed this:

"And may you have the power to understand, as all God's people should, how wide, how long, how high and how deep his love really is. May you experience the love of Christ, though it is so great you will never fully understand it." Ephesians 3:18-19

Attainable, yet unattainable. A goal within reach that we will never fully reach. How can that be? Paradox. But paradise. A love that goes beyond what we could ever experience from anyone else.

Let me try to reveal it further.

Ephesians 1:4-5 says, "Long ago, even before he made the world, God loved us and chose us in Christ to be holy and without fault in his eyes. His unchanging plan has always been to adopt us into his own family by bringing us to himself through Jesus Christ. And this gave him great pleasure."

Before he even made the world, God had planned to be born in a barn. Before he spoke the cosmos into existence, he was thinking of *you*. He knew that we would leave him. He knew we would choose our own way, that we would need help to break free from the bondage of sin. He knew that we couldn't do it on our own.

So, he emptied himself (Philippians 2) of all his rights as God and became like a servant. Like one of us. So that through his sinless life, and his victory over sin and death, we could live the life that He had planned for us...*even before he made the world.*

The part we most often miss in all of that is how God did it. I don't mean the deep theological discourse on the propitiatory ramifications of the salvific events on Golgotha. (I did learn *something* at Bible college...) I mean we miss his *joy!* He actually *wanted* to come. He *wanted* to be held in a young mother's arms. To be fed by her. To have his diapers changed by her. To grow up in the awkward body of an adolescent. To hear the taunts of the other kids. To feel the pain of a scraped knee. To know the hurt of words thrown carelessly around. To even know the sting of death. (Some think he lost his father, Joseph, at a fairly early age.)

Knowing all of that...it says that this plan, "gave him great pleasure."

That blows me away.

We all know John 3:16. It's at all the football games. It's graffitied on overpass bridge supports on the highway. It's memorized by anyone who's ever been near a Bible.

"For God so loved the world that he gave his only son, so that whoever believes in him will not perish, but have eternal life."

But what does verse 17 say? Something rather important, wouldn't you think? Following the verse that sums up all of human history? It has to be at least close in significance. Yet, when I ask the question of any group of believers, the raised hands are much more sparse than for the previous verse.

"God did not send his son into the world to condemn it, but to save it."

How often do we thank God in amazement for his gift of salvation, our ticket to heaven, but then as we continue in our life, we begin to fear failing him. We feel we must continue to improve, or risk losing his love. Perhaps in some sort of celestial dog house. On God's bad side.

But Romans assures us this is not the case. God's love toward us—his non-condemnation—is not a once, so-we-can-get-in-and-turned-around kind of love. It is constant. It is for all time. It was long before the world was formed. It was even while we were still his enemies. Listen to the following lines from Paul's letter to the Romans.

Romans 3:23-24

For all have sinned, and fall short of the glory of God and are justified freely by his grace through the redemption that came by Christ Jesus. (NIV)

Romans 5:7-11

Now, no one is likely to die for a good person, though someone might be willing to die for someone who is especially good. But God showed his great love for us by sending Christ to die for us while we were still sinners. And since we have been made right in God's sight by the blood of Christ, he will certainly save us from God's judgment. For since we were restored to friendship with God through the death of his son while we were still his enemies, we will certainly be delivered from eternal punishment by his life. So now we can rejoice in our wonderful new relationship with God—all because of what our Lord Jesus Christ has done for us in making us friends of God.

Romans 8:1

So now there is no condemnation for those who belong to Christ Jesus.

Romans 8:31

What can we say about such wonderful things as these? If God is for us, who can ever be against us?

Romans 8 continues to say that we can never lose God's love. We never did anything to earn it in the first place. God doesn't love me because I am such a good songwriter. Or a singer. Or a web-page builder. Or a good husband, father, son, brother, neighbor…

That's not why he loves us.

God loves me just because he made me. I was messed up. I still am. But he knew he could fix it. He came. And it gave him great pleasure.

That is the story of Christmas. God became man. The eternal lived in the temporal. He lived just like we did, yet was faultless. And in that way, he paid our way to eternal life.

Jesus said, "And this is the way to have eternal life, to know you the one true God, and Jesus Christ whom you have sent."

That's it. His offer is good to any who would accept it. Life like it oughta be. With the one who invented it. Made right by that same one. Made perfect.

The bumps will still come. Death still has a limp grasp on us. Just look at the catastrophic death that people are dealing with in Asia from the recent tsunami disasters. People will still lose their jobs, their spouses, their houses. But God came. He proved once and for all that he loves us, by not only coming to endure life in a messed up world, but by willingly dying for me. For you.

If God is for you, then who—or what—could ever be against you?

Think about these things as we close 2004. Think about his love that surpasses understanding.

"When I think of the wisdom and scope of God's plan, I fall to my knees and pray to the Father, the Creator of everything in heaven and on earth. I pray that from his glorious, unlimited resources he will give you mighty inner strength through his Holy Spirit. And I pray that Christ will be more and more at home in your hearts as you trust in him. May your roots go down deep into the soil of God's marvelous love. And may you have the power to understand, as all God's people should, how wide, how long, how high, and how deep his love really is. May you experience the love of Christ, though it is so great you will never fully understand it. Then you will be filled with the fullness of life and power that comes from God.

"Now glory be to God! By his mighty power at work within us, he is able to accomplish infinitely more than we would ever dare to ask or hope. May he be given glory in the church and in Christ Jesus forever and ever through endless ages. Amen." (Ephesians 3:14-21)

I Call You Friends

Jan 24th, 2005

I was listening to one of our many Wayne Jacobsen audio MP3s today, and he was talking about how in his many travels and speaking engagements, he loves to spend time with the folks there before he gets up to speak. The conversations are always open and genuine and great. Then he is introduced as the speaker, and there are gasps of, "*That's* who that was?!?" and the embarrassed attendee will approach him afterward with apologies for not knowing *who* he was.

In fact, they were more right when they didn't think they knew.

He made the comparison then that I was already making in my head (which is probably what he wanted me to be doing…) That is like Jesus. Jesus is God. But he was also a man, and as a man, he got to spend face-to-face time with the ones he created and loves—without them cowering in fear of the Holy and Awesome God.

How funny is that?! The disciples were hanging out with God…and still found time to bicker, to doubt, and even to have fun and laugh. There was no fear…there was "equal" relationship.

It seems that is what God is longing for. To return to Eden. Where he had an open and amazing relationship with the ones he created. Jesus made that possible again. As a man, without people knowing (*really* knowing) who he was, he was able to have genuine relationship with everyone.

Have you noticed that since we have figured out that Jesus was God, we have re-deified him? We have created a religion to surround him and separate him from us? We paint halos on him. We have put him back in his "proper" place as God.

Granted, Jesus is to be worshipped as God. He is God. But I think we see that he also wanted to eat and drink with friends at weddings. He also wanted to hang out with the low-lifes in society. He just wants relationship with us. When we didn't know who he was, that was even more possible.

If we *really* knew who he was, it would be better still.

God is so much more accessible than we let ourselves believe. He is not put off by our sin. We are not untouchable. (Look at all the "untouchables" whom Jesus physically touched while he was here.) We are the object of his affection, the reason he put on skin and died.

It's time to remember, rather than subjects in his Kingdom, or slaves who call him Master…he calls us friends.

SECTION 2

Doing Life Together

Our Place In History

Sep 4th, 2004

Did you ever think about who is coming after you? How your life will affect not just those in your path today, but those 3 or even 4 generations from now? The small things we choose and do today could have far more impact tomorrow than they do today.

I was reading Matthew today, just for fun. If you recall, the very beginning of the book is the "boring" genealogy part. I'm with you. It's really kind of boring. But look at what I read, and take a different look at it with me for a second.

Matthew 1:5-6

> Salmon had Boaz (his mother was Rahab),
> Boaz had Obed (Ruth was the mother),
> Obed had Jesse,
> Jesse had David,
> and David became king.

If you remember the stories of these folks, they are quite varied, and may seem insignificant even to us, and we already know the rest of the story. So, as they were living their lives, I wonder if they may have also felt somewhat regular, or average, perhaps even insignificant.

But think about them. Boaz was the son of Rahab. Rahab was a prostitute. Do you know any "upstanding" prostitutes? Any prostitutes who have a major impact on history? Not usually. But Rahab did. Because she had a respect for God that transcended her fear of men. She risked her life to do the right thing. She helped God's people, when she could have turned them over to their enemy.

And God rewarded her.

Not only in her lifetime, but He gave her a child. She named him Boaz. We meet Boaz in the book of Ruth. Ruth (also mentioned in these verses) was the woman who lost her husband, and even her brother-in-law and her father-in-law.

She could have been completely disparaged in life. But she was not. Instead, Ruth chose to put other people above herself and stayed with her mother-in-law to make sure that she was taken care of and loved. Very cool move. Probably seemed like a small thing for the most part to Ruth, but the right thing nonetheless.

So, when Naomi decides to return to her home town, Ruth decides to leave her life to follow her mother-in-law, and while there ends up meeting Boaz. Boaz, an older gentleman, takes kindly to young Ruth (I believe he was even a relative of Naomi) and ends up marrying Ruth.

And Obed was born.

Not much more is said about Obed. But this is my point.

Just a few cool, short stories. One was of a prostitute who honored God by her faith. Another of a widow who honored God by honoring her husband's mom. And God gave her a baby. A baby, who grew up to become a father. The father of Jesse. Again, not much said about his life.

But Jesse had a son. He had several sons. One of them was named David.

And David became King.

What a statement! From two lives that made at least one great choice for God (and at least for Rahab, several *bad* choices) to KING. And not just any King. David was a man after God's own heart. He led Israel (by God's hand) to be a powerful and peaceful nation. (Peace from enemies at least—not necessarily peace *FOR* their enemies.)

And I would bet that David's great-grandparents had something to do with that. They likely told stories of how they had to choose to honor themselves, or to honor God. And how when they chose to honor Him, God honored them. And that was passed on to the generation after them. And to the next. And to the next.

What are we doing today that will affect our great-grandchildren? Who will our descendants touch with their choices. What may seem small and insignificant today may have worldwide effects tomorrow. We can't know. We don't really need to. We just need to live each day loving God with all that we are and loving the people he puts in our path.

Could be that by me loving Ian, Alex or Kirsten, and sharing my life with our Father with them, that they will pass that on to their kids, who will pass it on to their kids, who will pass it on to their kids…

And they may become king.

Amazing.

So live today to the fullest. Do what is right. Love mercy, and walk humbly with your God. And you never know how God will use your good choices for him to change the future.

Age To Age

Sep 26th, 2004

I saw decades of time pass in only a few steps through Wegman's Market today.

First, as I was hurrying through the store to grab some diapers for our third child, Kirsten, I noticed a young couple apparently discussing which variety of bread they might need to take home. The first thing I noticed was how *young* they looked. (I *am* getting old!) Upon further (albeit quick) study, they appeared to be newlyweds. Just trying to figure out the new experience of shopping for groceries together.

I started thinking about when Jen and I were first married, and we were trying to figure out life together as one. Coming to a consensus on how we were going to do things wasn't always easy. But the coolness of time passed is that only the fond rememberings remain.

My next thoughts drifted to wondering if that was really what we looked like back then. Young, inexperienced, bewildered. Probably. It's fun to think you know what you're doing as you go along in life, but usually once you get far enough ahead to see clearly behind you, you realize that it was only wishful thinking. I assume that only continues to increase along the way.

So, I smiled at our naivety. At our inexperience. At our youthfulness.

And then I realized that I was staring at them, so I moved on.

Then, only a few paces further, I passed a man who was probably in his 70s. Perhaps even his 80s. (I hope he doesn't read this book, or if he does, that he doesn't mind me thinking him older than he is!) We exchanged smiles, and I kept on toward my diaper goal.

But then the time-warp thing happened again. I imagined me after living some 40 more years. 133% more than what I have already lived. What experiences must I have had? What challenges? What decisions must I have faced? What trials have gone into the wrinkles on my face? What joys have sustained me through them?

And I wondered what he thought of me. Forty years from now, will I look at the 30 year old father of 3 walking through Wegman's in search of diapers, and think back fondly to the days when I thought I had a good grasp on life. When I had a handle on life as I knew it. When I had youthful naivety. Longing for the freshness of that life, but relishing the wisdom that has come from all these years of experience. And the peace that has come with that.

Someday, perhaps I will be that man. And I will pass the young father, and smile. I will again pass the newlyweds…and smile. I will pass the new grandparents, and smile. I will hold the time-weathered hand of my wife of some 5 decades, and smile at where God has brought us.

For now, I will enjoy the current age. Thanks God for today. For the richness of the past and the hope of the future. You rock!

From age to age.

What World Are You In?

July 31st, 2004

We were watching the Democratic National Convention last week. There were some good points made during the several nights of speeches. Many I did not agree with, but many valid points as well. My parents are Super Republicans. I am not sure there was one thing they agreed with during the convention! Those things are both true. I'd also say that the majority of the folks we hang out with would lean toward the GOP as the GOP is the more conservative of the parties. I will admit, if I have a political paradigm, that is it.

So, with that paradigm, I was watching the DNC and noticed how lost in the Democrat world everyone was! It was *so* crazy! They kept saying things as though they were absolute fact, and…well, they just aren't.

Mostly, they would incorrectly state the views/beliefs of "the other" party. (Like, almost villianizing the "evil conservatives" of the GOP.) Or, they would say things like, "We need to restore trust in the white house." As though it were gone? And, "We need to become a united country again, and work hard to repair our image in the international community." As though we are not? As though it needs repair?

I am not sure who they are hanging out with, but it was pretty obvious that they are part of a homogenous group of people. They really think that NO ONE trusts this president. That *EVERYONE IN THE WORLD* hates the U.S. and can't wait for that bumbling Texan to be out of the White House. They really believe we are not united because they are surrounded by the nay-sayers.

We see the same thing in churches actually. Oft times the church can become its own little world. Its own kingdom. Where you almost lose touch with reality because everything you do is centered around the programming and schedule of your church. And that's particularly sad because we're supposed to help the world, not lose touch with it.

That is definitely an easy thing to do though. We are where we are. That is human nature. We are good at being self-focused. But life is bigger than the "perimeter of me" (a line from a song by that title written by Tasha Golden of

Dividing The Plunder). We can think we are seeing the whole picture, but often we are not. And those folks at the convention were a perfect example.

So I encourage you…take an opportunity to walk in someone else's shoes. See things through someone else's eyes. Those words are easier to say than to do, but really, could be "eye opening".

And you may just get a glimpse of what world *you* are in.

The Others

Dec 4th, 2004

Part of our business is paying attention to, and then doing what other people want. We are in marketing and sales. We have a product that we need people to want enough to plop down some of their hard-earned money in exchange for said product. So we definitely need to be concerned with what others are thinking (about us).

Also, the nature of our product lends itself to a vast smorgasbord of subjectivity. Our abilities are scrutinized, even our hearts, as the music is put on a public platter for consumption and either praise or ridicule…or worse yet, indifference.

All that said, why do I still care about what other people think?

This weekend, at the big Michigan craft show I have thought many times about all of the various opinions regarding our presence there. We're too loud. We're too Christian. We're too mellow. We're too upbeat. We're not loud enough. We haven't mentioned enough that people can get CDs at our table. We've mentioned that *too* much.

And the wrestling match continues until the scales balance in my favor, and I *feel* appreciated and wanted. But that is a precarious peace as the winds of people's opinions change direction faster than a Buffalo Bills winning streak.

So even with the knowledge of that truth, I persist in my incessant quest to be liked. On the surface it seems to be for financial gain. We need money. I need to be liked in order to sell stuff in order to make money…or so it would seem. But, perhaps it even runs deeper. Perhaps I am still quite preoccupied with me?

Isn't that just it? Doesn't our focus on others' opinions mean that we are essentially preoccupied with ourselves? Not narcissistic, where we are oblivious to others completely. Rather, we care a lot about what our image is, about who people think we are. About what they think of us.

I already know. I am a child of God. Full heir of all the stuff my Dad has. Now, not later. I am completely loved before the creation of the world. At God's great pleasure. And I am heaven's masterpiece, created anew in Christ Jesus.

That's who I am.

Did you notice that none of that relates to other people? The church is nice, and in fact, God openly shows his deep love for the church (all of those who belong to him, collectively) by calling her his bride in anticipation of the wedding. There is a level of emotional love and infatuation there that reveals the depth of passion with which God loves us. Not just a commitment to a forlorn spouse…but the eager anticipation of union with the One who is loved more than all. That is his love for his church.

But do you notice that his love is for me? God so loved the world that he gave his only son that whoever believes in him will not perish. That's not for a group. That has nothing to do with anyone else. That is for me. And throughout Scripture we see glimpses of his deep and personal love for *each* of us. It's amazing.

So since we know that, why do we focus so much on what others of God's children perceive us to be? Or better stated, our perception of what others perceive us to be?

God definitely made us relational. That is a big part of it. In a relationship, you do care about how you are perceived. Often we take that too far, but I know I want Jen to think positively of me, and very little makes me feel more loved than Jen's genuine expressions of affection for me, whatever forms they may take. Not out of obligation, but a real love for me…even with all my flaws.

We try hard then to ensure that the others we do life with are happy with us, that they know they are loved, and we want to know also that we are loved in return. Quite a selfish love, but, we are quite selfish at our core.

That is where Jesus is so amazing. He was able to somehow love selflessly. Eyes off of self, only driven by his affection for every single person he came across. Even the people who hated him, and whom he harshly accused (the Pharisees). We see his love for them when he blasts them, then proceeds to lament at how they would not accept his offer of protection. "Jerusalem, how I have longed to take you under my wing like a hen with her chicks." At the great cost of himself, Jesus loved deeply. Just because he did.

That is where we are to care about others. Not about what they think of us. Not about how we can be served by others, or relationship with them. Not falling into the trap of comparing ourselves to others. But really care about them. Not ourselves.

Jesus said that we can fit all of the Old Testament into one sentence. That's a good deal for those of you who do not like to read. (I am fairly certain that none of you reading this fall into that category as I can be quite verbose at times…) He said that the Law and the Prophets could be summed up in this, "Love the Lord your God with all you are (my paraphrase) and love your neighbor as yourself."

That is it right there.

And I don't really think that's a command. Sometimes it can feel like that, but I really believe that if we understand the depth of the love God has for us, and we live in that each day, we will love the others around us just like we have been loved. We won't seek to win their approval. We won't be afraid of them. We won't compare ourselves to them, in a self-loathing way. We will know the Truth of our Father's love for us…an unchanging constant…and that will flow into the lives of others that are around us. They will know that truth as a direct outflow of our relationship with the One who loves us most, and whose opinion really matters.

Live in God's love for you, and the Others will benefit from your gain.

Audience

Oct 17th, 2004

We sang at a coffee house tonight. We have done that plenty of times before. But this night there was an audience, and there was not an audience. That in itself was not extremely out of the ordinary, but it gave me something to think about.

At times tonight, I could sense that though the room was full of people, we did not have an audience. Yes, had we stopped, there would have been an absence of music that would have been missed…eventually. And in that way, we may have had an audience. But mostly, we were singing to the air.

And in general, that does not make for the best performances of songs.

My rhythm gets sloppy. My fingering of the chords is less than stellar. I start to forget words as my mind wanders from topic to topic. I don't actually hit the note I intended to on occasion.

But, if for some reason, I catch a glimpse of a real audience, someone who is actually listening and even enjoying what they hear, the song improves a lot! Not just technically improved over the previous paragraph, but even better delivered. From the heart. For real.

Isn't that weird???

Tonight, after lots and lots of singing—and varying levels of audience—I opened my eyes (sometimes I overcome a lack of audience by just singing the songs to God…HE is my audience) and I saw a couple girls waiting in line for their coffee. To my amazement, they were paying attention! And smiling! And I actually noticed that the chorus of the song that immediately followed the discovery of that newfound audience was just better than many other tunes had been that night.

I think that is so odd.

For the most part it's odd because I do *NOT* do this because I want people to "look at me!" My personality is "DON'T look at me!" I have never been one to crave the limelight.

But I guess, since music is meant to be communicated, it needs an audience. And when one arrives, the level automatically is raised.

It is possible that something like that might occur in anything that is done for other people. Sometimes a thought of you crosses my mind when I write, and the writing is better for it. The more people I know are reading, the more energy I have to share my thoughts? Again, that is not my motivation for writing, perhaps just adds gas to the fire?

And don't you love to share something you have just created with the nearest person whom you think might care? Whether it's a kitchen creation, or a craft, or a fine-crafted piece of furniture, or a website, or a model train, or a brand new attic…we love to share our creations and our accomplishments.

It is an innate need, a desire, for acknowledgment of me. Not selfish, not self-absorbed, I don't even think it is unhealthy in any way. I think it's who God made us to be. Something in us wants to be worth something. And in a way, the things that we produce make us worth something. Too much value can easily be placed on those things produced, rather than our value being derived from who our Creator has said we are. But they do give us value nonetheless.

So the question I came to was, would I write and sing these songs, even with no audience (save God, of course)? Would I write anything I publish if not a soul would ever read them? Would the quality of my cooking diminish if I knew that no one but me would ever enjoy it?

I think so. And before you call me a fickle, immature, self-centered jerk, consider this with me again. This is not necessarily a bad thing.

We were made to serve others. God first, then other Servers. We actually improve our serve as there are Servers to be served. The audience *does* make a difference. The energy level does increase proportionate to the size or attention level of an audience.

So remember that next time you are invited to receive another Server's creation. Be it musical or lyrical or other-cal. You play an important role in that exchange—for both the Server and the Served.

Be an audience.

The Playboy Girl

Sep 3rd, 2004

We sang at a coffee house tonight in Clarence Center, NY—our old stomping grounds—and some friends we have not seen in a long time were there. (Marie, I'm going to put you in here by name since you said I didn't mention anything specifically about the last time we saw you guys...) It was great to see them and really cool that they came out to hear us.

The place was pretty busy for a Thursday night, and mostly teeming with teens. It appears to be a teen hang-out spot. That's cool. Except a bunch of these young teens were smoking and otherwise entwined in the world. They were playing the societal games of wearing the right clothes, having the right haircut, doing the right things, hanging with the right people...they were doing it all.

Actually, when I got there, I was really close to going up to this boy who could not have been more than 14 or 15, and telling him that it's illegal for him to smoke at his age. But that just felt very judgmental. Very finger-pointy. And I really think that's not how Jesus treated people.

I asked Jesus right there to help me that night to see people as he does. He's not *mad* at that boy for breaking the law, instead I would bet that he is more sad. Just hurting for him that he is choosing something he probably knows is bad. Most of us don't make bad choices because we're stupid. Often we make bad choices as a way to fit in. Jesus knows that, and loves us in spite of our weakness.

A little later, a young girl, again 14 or 15, joined the group. She was dressed to attract attention to herself. She wore tight jeans that don't come up very far, and a tight, low-cut, spaghetti-strap shirt that didn't go all the way down to her pants. And to top it all off, she wore a Playboy baseball cap and a Playboy belt. Both Jen and I saw this girl and were at first amazed, and then I began to remember what I had asked Jesus to help me see.

I imagine that she doesn't really like a magazine that flaunts women's bodies in ways they should not be flaunted. I would suspect that she just wants attention. She has found one way to get it. On several occasions, my eyes were inadvertently directed to the body parts she intended to receive the attention. And each time I was saddened for her.

Well, during one song, a group of the teens came up past us and into the coffee house (we were outside on the patio tonight) and she was one of them. They passed only a few inches from us. I smiled at each one as we sang, and when Playboy Girl passed, our eyes met.

For a moment, brief as it was, something connected. I don't remember what I was singing, but I remember thinking right afterward, "I hope she knows God's love even through that one eye-meeting." I never got to speak with her, but perhaps Jesus (who lives in ME!) did. Perhaps through the songs, or merely through a look of Jesus-love.

There are so many hurting, lonely, lost people in the world. Lots of them sit in churches on the weekends. Jesus makes that a lot better. His love is so much deeper than we can ever know. His attention is so much more satisfying than any teen-age boy looking at parts of your body that are not his to look at.

I pray that she knows the peace of his love tonight.

I pray you do too.

The Extras

Sep 24th, 2004

I was at a gas station the other day, just pumping some gas (for myself, not for other folks...I did not land a day job at the local gas station).

And I noticed something.

For one brief moment, I became part of another world.

There was a family there, pushing the stroller, with two other kids in tow. They were trying to manage a mob of small, energetic people. And as I watched and listened, I thought, "Hey, that's like us. That is us. We walk right through here, and there are people pumping gas when we walk by. Now *I* am the guy pumping gas in *their* world!"

And just then I realized that we are so egocentric. I am using that term in the philosophy sense, not the selfish, prideful, arrogant sense. That means, *I* am the center of my world. Everything revolves around me, and is perceived from my vantage point. Mostly, the people around us are just like extras in a movie. Insignificant filler in the story of my life.

But they're not. Till I was pulled out of my world and swept into theirs, the family walking by were the extras, not me. But then all of a sudden, from a different perspective, *I* was the extra.

I was no longer husband to Jen, father to Ian, Alex and Kirsten. I was no longer a musician, writer, web-designer. I was no longer Tom and Shirley's son, and Tara's brother. I was just a guy pumping gas.

Isn't that so odd? The following day at Wal-Mart, I began seeing people for who they really are. There are a lot of people at Wal-Mart. Each person has a rich past, and a full present. They are someone's Dad, Mom, Grandma, Grandpa, son, daughter, friend, boss, partner, pastor, teacher, doctor, etc.

And yet to me, they are extras.

I won't have the opportunity to be part of any of their worlds. Perhaps some. But likely, they will remain in a way, extras. But, I would like to remember that gas-station experience where for a moment, the world was not my world.

What a world it would be if there were no extras. If we realized the fullness of everyone we run into at a gas station. That is only a piece of the world God knows. He knows each of us intimately. Every detail. Every relationship. All that we are. More than anyone else.

Now that is amazing. Six billion people on this planet and God knows everyone of them like they were his best friend...and better.

Quite a perspective God has on this world, eh?

4:58

Sep 24th, 2004

Have you ever been squeezed for time, with lots to do and a deadline to meet? Errands to run, kids to feed, people to meet. And you're pretty much staying on top of things, you know when the post office closes, and you have *just* enough time to get there if you hurry.

Closing time is posted as 5:00pm. When you arrive, your clock says 4:58, so you know you're OK. You just have one package to mail.

You get out of your car, and head in only to see the window is being closed! You check your watch again—4:58. But the clock on the wall says 5:06pm. WHAT?!?!?

That frustrating scenario has happened to me far too often, and yesterday I think it happened to the lady coming in as I was going out of the post office. I saw the window being closed by the quite ominous barrier they bring down at closing time, and just for fun, checked my receipt to see what time their computer said from my sale not 30 seconds ago.

4:58.

It said, 4:58pm. Two official minutes left before closing time, but the window was coming down in a hurry.

OK, so turning the clock ahead on the wall is silly, and a cheesy way to honor your posted closing times, but when you close *early*, there is the greater problem with Americans these days.

We are not here to serve other people. We are just earning a paycheck, and that's it. The mentality is, "Get as much out of it for me as a I can." Longer breaks, come in right on time or just a bit late, leave *JUST* a bit early. It's all about me.

Ever been to a Chinese restaurant? (That is a rhetorical question…) Ever notice that for the most part, you are the important person there? Not them. The focus is properly placed on serving and honoring other people above yourself. Jesus said that's a better way to do life, and I think everyone outside of America gets that.

But we close at 4:58. We set our clocks fast. Cut every corner. All just to serve ourselves.

I want us to be more like small town USA. Even if we don't stay open late for one person who needs a break on an overwhelmingly busy day, at least we could honor our posted hours!

Do nothing out of selfish ambition or vain conceit, but in humility consider others better than yourselves. (Philippians 2:3—NIV)

Some might say, "Greg…it's just a job! Seriously. Do the consider others thing *AFTER* work…" But I think the best place for Jesus to be seen is…everywhere. In everything we do. Every place we are.

Love God with all you've got, and love his people—even consider them better than yourself—and life will go well for you.

And everyone around you.

Love

I was listening to a song on the way to play some basketball this morning, and the words just slammed me in the face with the "power of love" (and no, I don't mean the Huey Lewis version.)

Listen…

What I Would Say

She was a lovely girl, a charming brown-eyed beauty
You were the bright young man who swept her off her feet
The high school class ring soon became a wedding band
And you went off to sail the seas for Uncle Sam
But they say it was the demon in the bottle
That took you far away never to return
And you never knew your son would be my father
And now sometimes I think about you and I wonder
If I could talk to you what words would I choose

OK, so that part is the set up, but here's the part that WHACKED me. Oh wait. This song is written by Steven Curtis Chapman to his Grandpa, whom he never met. OK, now, here's the chorus (and the rest of the song):

I would say I wish I could have known you
And I would say I wish you would have stayed
But most of all I would say I forgive you

I know your love was strong I read it in your letters
I read how hard you tried to break free from the chains
I know we all could say how you should have done better

And wear our anger and resentment like a fetter
But that's why I would say this to you if I could

I would say I wish I could have known you
And I would say I wish you would have stayed
But most of all I would say I forgive you

I'd love to tell you how the lovely girl you married
She's been my hero and a treasure to us all
I know you'd be proud of the way your name's been carried
These are things I would love to tell you if I could

I would say I wish I could have known you
And I would say I wish you would have stayed
But most of all I would say I forgive you

I wish you were here to hear what I would say

Wow. Seriously. That was not what I was expecting to hear or think about this morning. But emotionally stirred inside, I said out loud to God, "Love is SO powerful!"

It is amazing. The way that it can melt us. Just to hear this story about a guy who messed up his life and his family's life, and then to hear the forgiveness—driven by love…it's amazing.

We know that kind of love through Jesus giving up his life in heaven to DIE on a large piece of wood…to say "I love you…and I forgive you…". And every time we see that happen in life, whether we are the forgiver, forgivee or just an observer, we see the power of love in action all over again.

A friend of mine messed up some stuff recently. He's in a world of hurt. And really, he is in *more* hurt because of the way he is being treated about it. There is some pretty nasty stuff being thrown at him that he doesn't really deserve. And unfortunately, it's all by other Jesus-followers. What if, instead of righteous indignation (or perhaps, self-righteous would be a better label?)…what if…just maybe…some of the above forgiveness was shown? What if the other Jesus-followers would use the power of love to melt the broken and/or sinful and/or stubborn hearts of everyone involved, and see healing and restoration happen?

What if…

I am just blown away by the power of love today. (And unfortunately I'm going to be singing that all day, too!! "That's the *POW*er oooof love!" [Cue the 80s synths…])

I hope you get a chance to melt someone's heart today with the power of love. In forgiveness, in mercy, in compassion, in affection, in encouragement, in praise…however you do it, just do it.

The Church

March 22nd, 2004

Just been thinking again about what the church really is. This past week while I was in a mostly empty church building, I was reminded that it is not about any of the programming we do (sorry to you worship planners out there...) it is so much about *being* the church. The group of people who are extra-noticeable because of their changed lives. How they love each other, and do life together with a bond that's stronger than family. A commitment to engendering in each other that fullness of life that Jesus said he came to give us.

We are a part of so many churches, we see so many great things churches are doing to try and connect people with The One who loves them, and even to connect them with each other and to reach out to everyone around us. But so often, our energy is poured into organizing such things so that it is an efficient process. And there I think we miss the point.

The church does not have a product (such as a trained and equipped disciple). The church is a living organism. The body of Christ, in fact. Jesus is the head. He gives us directions, we listen and follow, and do our part. (That does not mean, necessarily, that we should listen for where he wants us to serve, like, the nursery, or teaching 3rd grade Sunday school, or as a member of the board, or whatever...)

What it does mean is, we get to love each other, and those around us, like He did. As though we were his hands and feet. Take care of our body (feed it, clean it, groom it, rest it, etc...) and then use it to go love others.

It might be as simple as just "being" the church instead of "doing" church. We are oh so good at doing church these days. We have books, seminars, speakers, retreats, conventions, even colleges that have professors whose entire lives are devoted to training people in how to "do" church.

I am in a small group that is good at being the church. We do life together. We are always there to help each other. No one is left out. We are accountable to each other. We share life's joys and hardships. Good stuff.

That's the church.

Not the building. Not the programs. Not the staff. Not the budget. Not the outreach events. Not the mission trips. Not the worship services. Not the small group programs. Not the children's ministries. Not the big Easter productions. Not the potluck dinners. (Actually…that might come close…)

It is the sharing of life together by believers. Every bit of it. Not once a week, or even twice. But genuine caring, relationship-oriented, living, breathing, thriving life-together.

That will change the world.

Our Mission

Nov 23rd, 2004

Do you know that Christians actually get tired of being Christians?

I don't mean the simplicity of being a child of God, I mean all of the stuff we do that makes us feel like Christians.

We get up early to have "quiet times", faithfully reading the same Bible passages we have read many times before, mining for truths that we may not have seen before. We pray harder. We take on more ministry opportunities. We fill our schedule with as much of the programming at our church as we are able. We even help in the nursery at church!!

Even deeper than that, there's the constant battle of trying to beat down our sinful nature. To win a battle that is not winnable. To defeat the tendencies we have toward sin, and to always do what is right and righteous.

It is the constant struggle to prove that we are worthy of the Cross. Of God's unfathomable love.

And that occasionally grows wearisome.

At times, we can sustain it. For a week. For a month. Even the best part of a year. But most of us can not, and so we settle for a guilt-ridden life of not measuring up to God's standards. We read the law and know that we *should* do that...but we can not. And so we end up with frustration after frustration, repentance after repentance, hoping for the goodness of God's grace to cover our mistakes up to now, and weary from the thought of the next ones to come...perhaps only minutes from your current confession.

Not all Christians live in fear, but I think most do not get to live in the freedom of God's love. We fight and struggle to do what is right, and we work so hard to spread the good news of Jesus.

Good news? Have you been reading? Does the above sound like good news? Doing a lot of stuff you don't really want to do all the time, even though you can't which just leaves you feeling beaten down and worthless until you come to another confession time and start it all over again? It is all based on a works-oriented, task-driven way of relating to God.

He is after all, God. He calls the shots. He gives and takes away. Who are we to have any say in what we do or don't do. Christians through the ages have told us what God likes and what he doesn't, and I have even read it in His word…He likes it when we're good, and doesn't like it when we're bad. A bit simple, but isn't that basically it?

I don't think so.

We have been reading **He Loves Me**, by Wayne Jacobsen, and I have been really rethinking who God, my Father, is. To be completely honest, there are not many books that make me completely rethink anything. I am a thinker. That's what I do. I love to think deeply on things. Any things. But especially anything having to do with God. And so, this book has simply amazed me at its simple look at the love that God has for us.

He has taken us through the parable we call the Prodigal Son. He contends that the story is not really about the son, he is only one of two. The story in fact is about a father who loves unabashedly *both* of his quite different sons. One wild and selfish, the other self-righteous and indignant. Both are loved completely. Then he obviously uses the cross as a picture of God's love. Which I have known, but he has made me seriously rethink some of the motivations of God for the cross. It was not just to appease his judgment. It was to defeat sin, and its hold on me. To completely defeat sin and death. It was out of love that God himself allowed his life to be taken (no one could take it from him) so that he could defeat death and sin's hold on us all. He did all of this before we were even born, and before anyone really asked for it. (Ephesians 1 says his plan was formulated before the creation of the world.)

This unstoppable love of the supreme God for me has fascinated me these past few weeks, and especially as we have read through this book. If you do not own a copy, they are available at Amazon.com, or Wayne's website (www.lifestream.org) Please do go buy one, or two. I make no money from that, I just want you to read it.

And it has made me wonder why we Christians do what we do. We have some missionary friends who are tired. They have worked so hard and given their all to help people in a foreign land know the Truth, the Way and the Life. But they are tired. Weary.

I know preachers who endure endless meetings, discussions, politics, maneuvering, power struggles, late-nights, and so much more in the name of serving their King. And they fight to keep going just because they don't know what else to do. People need to know, right?

I know so many in full-time ministry who are empty, and dry, and wondering if it is worth going on, and if they are not exhibiting that externally, they are battling that internally. And why? Because they are trying too hard to do something for God, instead of letting Him do something in them.

I think the key is we have forgotten who God is. We have "a form of Godliness, but deny its power." We work so hard because we are pretty sure we have to keep up our end of the bargain, and in doing so, we often miss the *real ministry* that God has placed right in front of us.

That might be our family. That might be our neighbors. That might be someone we happen to meet in the parking lot of our local grocer. Whomever that might be, we are so busy building up our kingdoms (our churches) that we often miss The Kingdom happening right around us. We create our own world to serve by building a building to house all of the great programs to attract people so that we might reach as many as possible. There are so many details to manage, so many people to care for, and so few to do the things that need to be done, so we have to recruit more. It is an endless process.

And God did not call us in Scripture to any of it.

What did Jesus say was the greatest commandment? The thing he *most* wants us to do? He quoted Deuteronomy where it says we should "Love the Lord your God with all your heart, all your mind, all your soul and all your strength. The second is just like it, love your neighbor as yourself." That's it. We have no commands to create elaborate structures by which we may hopefully communicate the teachings of Jesus to many people in our local area. We are just told to love them. That's it.

Love is a crazy English word. We say it is a choice. Has nothing to do with emotions. The Love of God (agape, in Greek) is a conscious choice to do what is in the best interest of the one being loved. Sounds great, eh? NO! That is not what made God hang on a cross. That is not the love of the father in the Incredible Father story…that is heartless and calculated, obligatory love. That is not the love God has for us, and not how he wants us to love him or our neighbor.

He wants us to long to be with him. To relish the thought of helping out a friend or neighbor. To bubble with joy at the opportunity to share what God has given you, just because He has.

That's not always easy, but it's easier when we are not tired from trying so hard. It's easier when we get up in the morning and follow God's plan for us, instead of creating our own agenda.

I probably have lost a lot of you by now. I am sorry for that. I don't mean to. Nor do I mean to in any way condemn anyone who is reading this for not doing anything I have mentioned the "right" way.

I do think we are missing out on the fullness of life in Jesus (he said he came that we might have life to the full—John 10:10) and mostly that is because we are trying so hard to attain it, instead of resting in the fact that He has already given it to us. We just need to live it with Him.

I intend to re-read the whole Bible over the next while, reading it with eyes open to God's incredible love for me. The love that says I am his child, not just a subject in his Kingdom. The love that says I am his bride, and he is the groom. The love that says he sings over me. I will definitely be posting thoughts along the way as I do.

I hope you know his love for you. Romans 8:31 says if God is for us, who (or what) can be against us. That question is posed because the first part is so unmistakably true. God *is* for us.

Max Lucado played with the phrase once. Say it with the inflection on all the different words. They are all true. And they all hold a different and amazing meaning.

God is for us. The almighty. Creator of heaven and earth. *HE* is for us.

God *is* for us. Today. Not once, a long time ago. Not just when he died on the cross. Not just when we were good. He *IS* for us…now.

God is *for* us. He loves us. He is on our side. He is cheering us on, picking us up, constantly warmed by the thought of *you*.

God is for *us*. You and me. Not the special people. Not the "saints". Not the ones who love him the best. He is for *US*. All the time. Forever.

That is amazing.

I pray, as Paul did, that "out of his glorious riches he may strengthen you with power through his Spirit in your inner being, so that Christ may dwell in your hearts through faith. And I pray that you, being rooted and established in love, may have power, together with all the saints, to grasp how wide and long and high and deep is the love of Christ, and to know this love that surpasses knowledge—that you may be filled to the measure of all the fullness of God." *Ephesians 3:16-19*

Know, as I am learning, that you are so incredibly loved. As you are, not as you need to be. Forever.

That is our purpose for being. To share in that love. THAT…is our mission.

They Will Know We Are Christians By Our Love

Oct 28th, 2004

By this all men will know that you are my disciples, if you love one another. (John 13:35—NIV)

Perhaps you have heard this verse before? Or perhaps you have sung the song, "They will know we are Christians by our love, by our love..."

It is interesting to me how many other ways we try and label ourselves Christians. How many things we think make us "Christians" or, Jesus' disciples.

There are bumper stickers, those little fishies, t-shirts, jewelry, hand bags, wall hangings, pictures frames, signs, and all sorts of things to adorn your walls or to adorn you that say to everyone, "I AM A CHRISTIAN!"

There are buildings with tall steeples, and huge crosses, and statues, and large marquees with generally amusing messages proclaiming to the world what we believe, and who we are.

We have statements of faith and pages of doctrine to tell people who we are.

We have morals and practices and disciplines and prohibitions that define who we are.

We have our own music, our own TV channels, our own music festivals, our own coffee houses, and even our own skate nights to set us apart from the world and declare who is our Master.

Yup! There's no mistaking it! With all of these very evident markings of a Christian, the world can not mistake where our allegiance lies, or the greatness of the one we follow!

Right?

Wrong.

Jesus said, by *THIS* everyone will know you are my disciples—that you follow me, that you reflect me—*if you love one another.*

There is no doctrine, no building, no set of rules, no list of disciplines, no amount of prohibitions that will demonstrate to the world who we are more than if we simply love each other. Really. Not fake demonstrations to catch the eyes of those around us, but true, simple, honest, heart-felt, generous, lavished-on love.

Why?

Because that is who our Leader is. Our Father is all of those things to all of us. So people will know we belong to him not by the rules we keep or the doctrine we teach, or even the clothes we wear. Those things are not the core of who our Father is. They will recognize him in our unabashed, unconditional, unrelenting love for each other.

So why do we work so hard on the other stuff? Perhaps because it's easier to keep a set of rules or to preach a doctrine than to actually give up time or money or other resources just to love another disciple. And love not only costs us those things, it also costs our comfort. We are vulnerable when we love the way our Father does.

Most all of the things I mentioned above are not bad, and generally do come from a life of following Jesus. But they are *so* secondary. If we do all of that, but don't exhibit love openly and wildly, it might still be hard for people to see Who we follow, or if they do, their picture of Him will be distorted.

They will know you are Jesus' disciples by your love.

Jesus did not make life hard for us. It is really simple. He summed up the whole Old Testament in these two lines: Love the Lord your God with all your heart, with all your soul, with all your strength, with all your mind. And love your neighbor as yourself.

When we learn that life is not about me, it sure gets a lot better.

And the world will too, as they see in us the visible demonstration of who our Leader—our Father—really is.

Professional Christians

June 10th, 2004

I just flipped through a flyer for an upcoming national christian convention. We are not going, but boy did the flyer make me feel like I should. Glossy, attractive photos of all the best and brightest the christian industry has to offer. All in one place!

And for a moment, I thought, "We should go!" But the next moment, I almost threw up.

Really. I understand that certain people are great at what they do, but do we believers really want to market and profit from our walk with Jesus? Fellow Christians being paraded around in big show after big show, complete with the consumer-oriented marketing and packaging?

Jesus was so not consumer-oriented. He was not flashy. He was impressive, but not flashy. When people tried to put him in the spotlight, he said, not yet. He is the one before whom every knee will bow and every tongue confess his supremacy.... but not yet.

But a bunch of what I see today in Christendom is about the spotlight. (See, we even have a name for the whole big show—Christendom. It's an organization, a business, a sub-culture...not just life lived in Jesus' steps.)

That convention brochure was. The spotlight on the talented pastor or worship leader is. The emphasis on whose teaching you like, or whose writing is better, or whom you most enjoy in worship...

It's not about us folks. It's just about a bunch of ratty misfits (though they may even appear different on the outside) pickin' up and following the God-man who offered his life in their place. It's not about how pretty we smile, or how well we say stuff, or how well we sing. It's about how well we live. Not on the stage. In our kitchen. In our backyard.

I never want to be a professional christian. I only want to know and follow Jesus, and talk to people along the way. But I am thankful that God has allowed me to help people and know the greatness of seeing Him work through me—without the glamour of the Professional Christians.

I walk a funny line here, since in a way, I am a professional Christian. Just not quite so glitzy. I do have a website, though. And you know what, we often are torn with whether we are doing the right thing or not. We don't like "the system" at all—Christendom and such—but we do love telling people about the freedom of life with Jesus, and that is one avenue to do that.

So for now, with mixed emotions, we continue. If anyone out there has any ideas, we are definitely open to them. I just want to be like Jesus, in every way.

And, I'm pretty sure Jesus was not a Professional Christian.

Voluntary Communism

Aug 24th, 2004

"Hello, my name is Greg, and I am a Trekkie."

"Hello, Greg!" answers the chorus of mostly unison voices.

OK, I admit it. My wife and I both watch several episodes a week, own most of the movies on DVD and VHS and we have almost every episode of The Next Generation on VHS cassettes from a video club collection. We are Trekkies, no doubt about it. We have not gone as far as the fake pointy ears yet. Although, we did get Ian a pair of pajamas that are a Star Fleet uniform...

Well, one of the cool things about Star Trek (that as most things on that show, would probably not work in reality) is the way they do commerce. There is no money, they all just "share" the resources they need. That's not always explained, but I think the general idea is, you work for the good of everyone. You do what you do for everyone else's benefit, and in return they do what they do for you. Seems to make at least theoretical sense.

In the past, we have mentioned the awesome simple church community we are part of with our neighbors and others. We are meeting again tonight, and all bringing pieces of a dinner so we can eat together. Very cool. Probably will end up doing that a bunch more as (1) it allows us more time together and (2) it's just the *BEST* way to hang out with folks—over shared food.

And the other day, a bunch of us went to an amazing local water park called "The Sprayground". It was quite funny to see how we all had each other's kids in each other's cars. We are just one big community! We shared our lunch stuff, our toys, just very cool in every way.

Then after that some of our friends watched our kids, while we took another friend's kid (getting confused yet?) to go get some groceries for some other friends who are struggling financially at the moment.

That was *so cool!* I wasn't going to write about that, because it's fun to just quietly do good stuff, but I really want to encourage you all to be wildly crazy generous like that! IT IS SO COOL! I had just spoken with our friend the night before, and she said that they were having a hard time even buying groceries.

After we got off the phone, I saw that we had some money in our "Kingdom Fund" (a portion of our income that we set aside for God to use when the opportunity comes up) and Jen agreed that we should stock their cupboards for them!

SO...we did! And it was so great!!! For everyone!!

And what do we expect in return? NOTHING! Not a thing! But what will probably happen? If we ever need something, who's going to help us? THEY ARE! OR, if not them, any of our other friends with whom we share life. (And of course, our super generous family! We both have parents who are incredibly generous!)

Point is, communism, in its good, albeit theoretical ways—works. If we all would use what God has given us to benefit others when they are in need, it will usually come back around. Jesus talked a bit about that. The early church did that. No one was in need. Everyone shared everything in common. And Jesus said whatever you "give up" in this life, you will receive 5, 10, 100-fold back in *THIS LIFE* and the life to come.

It is *way* better to give than to receive. And so if everyone did that, like the theory of communism (I think?) then we'd be set. Really. I don't mean like China, or North Korea, or Russia, or any of those models of communism which offer a mentality of stealing from the rich, keeping everyone poor and dependent on the government. I just mean this:

Acts 4:32

All the believers were one in heart and mind. No one claimed that any of his possessions was his own, but they shared everything they had.

Acts 2:44-47

All the believers were together and had everything in common. Selling their possessions and goods, they gave to anyone as he had need. Every day they continued to meet together in the temple courts. They broke bread in their homes and ate together with glad and sincere hearts, praising God and enjoying the favor of all the people. And the Lord added to their number daily those who were being saved.

Cool, eh?

More Effective?

Sep 12th, 2004

We came out of the coffee house last night refreshed and encouraged, and pumped full of wonderful confections. Life was good, the people were friendly, and we had just shared some really great stuff about the Kingdom and our God that hopefully encouraged everyone to enjoy life with Him even more.

While I was loading our van I noticed that a couple houses over I saw red and blue lights flashing on the side of a house, and my christian fun-night became almost empty.

I don't mean to say that it's not good to encourage each other. I really think we need to do that, and spend lots of time together loving each other and encouraging each other. We are the body of Christ, and we need to take care of our body.

But when I saw those lights, I immediately thought, "It's not about a night of fun in the basement of a church. It's about knowing who those people are who are hurting, who are trapped, who need to be loved and shown the love they already have from their Father."

We know a guy who just a few years ago had many visits from the police to his house. He has had a history with alcohol and the many negative things that it makes you do. But today he is one of the coolest guys I know. He is real, transparent, trying to figure out what God wants for him and his family, and just growing more and more like Jesus all the time.

And we are somehow responsible for that!

That is the crazy part right there. In the past, he and his wife have attributed their changed lives to us. That is so funny, because we didn't do anything! We didn't sit down and sing them a song, we didn't preach them a sermon, we didn't invite them to church (well, not much at least), and we certainly didn't go through the four spiritual laws with them.

I think we just loved them.

And isn't that what it's really about? What did Jesus do more? We read about days where he healed people all day long. He spent lots of time just taking care of people's physical and emotional needs. He just loved them, because he did.

I love that I get to sing to a room of Christians who can be encouraged and reminded that Jesus loves them so completely that they can be free to live life letting that love overflow to everyone around them.

But I also know that sometimes we catch it all before it overflows.

We need to *be* where we are. We need to be known in the community. We need to know and be known by our neighbors. By the people we work with. We need to have eyes open to whom God has placed in our immediate proximity and how we can share life with them.

So, when the police lights are flashing on the side of their house, we can help put pieces back together. Not as the judge, but as someone who understands and humbly loves because we have first been loved.

Just being available to love seems like a more effective way to be a part of the Kingdom.

So make some love connections out there, people! (And then love the folks He connects you with!)

Home Handy Repairman Jack

Sep 21st, 2004

Yesterday was Monday. My day off. I spent *ALL* of my day-off yesterday—my one day to relax and recharge for the week ahead, after a week full of 20 hr days—*in my attic!*

Actually, it started Sunday afternoon (which is often the beginning of our family/down time). I did take a break to watch most of the Bills game, though I was cleaning the kitchen and cooking dinner while I was doing that.

Needless to say, it was not a very relaxing "weekend".

But, I do have a great looking attic. It is nearly done. That is very, very cool.

And I figured something out.

My dad is Mr. Handy Andy. (His name is not Andy, that just rhymed...) He can, and does do any project he likes around the home. Even does stuff for other people. And, I think he figures I should do the same thing. If there's a home project, I need to get the tools and do it!

My father-in-law and brother-in-law are similarly minded I think. Well, perhaps my father-in-law is more of a mind to have his son do it. But that is just the sage wisdom that comes with age. Oh, and my neighbor and most of the members of our small group are Handy Randys...especially my neighbor. He is amazing. Really. He's kinda like MacGuyver. Even has duct tape.

But I am not. God has gifted me in other areas. I am skilled in other arenas. But I am not gifted, skilled, nor do I desire to be in the area of "craftsmanship" or whatever you want to call it.

And that's not a bad thing.

I noticed yesterday that for some weird reason, everyone is expected to be able to do their own home repair or home projects. That's why there's Home Depot and other such stores. If you own a home, you are supposed to know what's wrong (or be able to figure it out) and get yourself to the store and select just what you need from the 1004 options in one aisle and then install it with the greatest of ease with the somewhat cryptic instructions occasionally included with the box!

We don't think that way about anything else. When your tooth hurts, you don't grab the pliers and start diggin' (well, outside of West Virginia, I mean...) When your car is not working, you don't put on your coveralls and drive it into your garage with the hydraulic lift and get under there and check it out. (Well, OK, my neighbor does that too. But, remember, he's MacGuyver.) For most services we need performed, we talk to people who know what they are doing.

But, not for a leaking drain, or an attic project, or drywall, or most any home repair project. If you do, you are either wasting money, or lazy, or stupid or something.

I think part of my above perception is related to the folks God has put around me, who are quite masterful at all things involving power tools. But I do think that generally it is true. And I don't think that it should be.

I am quite good, I think, at graphic design and especially website design. It is easy and fun for me. Most of the people I mentioned before wouldn't know the first thing about a website. If they needed one, they would not think, "Well, I should figure out how to do this and do it myself!" No, they would pay someone (preferably me...) to do it for them.

I am also a decent musician (only by God's call and grace). I make CDs. None of the folks above who can create amazing things with their hands would even think of creating an album for public consumption. And they don't need to. Nor are they *expected* to.

But there's a different standard for the home owner.

I have another brother-in-law who is equally gifted in craftsmanship (equal to me, that is) and he is so often the butt of jokes regarding his skills with a hammer or measuring tape. Why? Do we make fun of you because you can't perform surgery? Or because you can't make a filling? Or because you can't create a website? Of course not!

We are all gifted in different ways. And mostly, I'd say we understand that. That is part of the beauty of God's world. We all have a place in it. Hopefully you are doing what you are gifted at, and you have a passion for it, and enjoy doing it. And hopefully it is adding to society. And, hopefully, people are not putting undue pressure on you to do things you are *NOT* gifted to do!!!

I decided yesterday that after this attic project any project my Dad would like to do for me would be received with gratitude. (I will even help him all he wants, but he must finish it!!!) If my neighbor wants to help me with something...rock on.

But I will not do any home repair or similar tasks on my own. My time is better spent paying someone who *knows* what they are doing. Next year, when we plan to do some work in our kitchen…I AM HAVING SOMEONE DO IT!

YEAH!!! I am feeling pretty good about my new-found freedom from the fetters of fraudulent expectations. (And feeling fairly fine from some fun use of alliteration, too!)

The Freedom Of Uniqueness

Oct 28th, 2004

"When religion is characterized by sameness, when faith is franchised, when the genuineness of our experience with God is characterized by its sameness to others' faith, then the uniqueness of God's people is dead, and the church is lost."

I have just begun reading another book at the suggestion of a friend who now resides in Seattle, WA. They told us about it last year, and I am finally getting around to reading it. The above quote from chapter one caught my eye.

We are currently in Las Vegas, NV, spending some time with friends here, and joining them for a time on their journey to a simpler church. It has been a long one, we joined them about 3 years ago, when they were well into the journey. And it has been so interesting to catch up every year and a half or so. We get to see how their view of who they are supposed to be as the Church has grown, how it has changed. And we share our insights as well from seeing how God is molding hearts and minds, and changing perspectives among his people everywhere.

And one of the most consistent challenges to the freedom of the simple church is the notion that there must be a sameness, a systematic processing of Christian life. The quote from Michael Yaconelli's book Dangerous Wonder rang quite true in that way.

One of the most common questions for proponents of a simple church philosophy of doing life together with other believers is, "How do you control doctrinal truth and moral behavior?" Inherent within that question is a false belief that we ever actually control anything that happens in the Church. We know that the head of the church is Jesus, but in our humanness we strive to put systems and safeguards in place so that in case God is perhaps busy elsewhere, there is a means by which we can maintain some sense of order and sameness. A sense of purity and a bedrock of doctrinal truth to stand on.

A friend wrote recently that nearly all heresies or cults actually originated in attempts to control what happened amongst the believers, rather than a freedom to let heresy run rampant.

We think that we are so very important to God's kingdom. That no one would hear the Good News if we did not work diligently to present it in a culturally relevant way. That people would fall away from the Kingdom if we did not have a regular set of teaching, and training, and service opportunities, and structured fellowship gatherings to keep them on the straight and narrow.

How arrogant. How demeaning. How presumptuous. How condescending.

We are each on an individual journey with God. At very different places in that journey. We did not all get there the same way, we will not all continue on the same path to the end. But we do often get the chance to share that with folks at a similar place. To encourage and be encouraged. To share what Jesus has taught us and to be taught by the unique experiences of others on this journey of faith.

We are each quite unique. Freedom to experience and understand God in the way He chooses to reveal himself to us is crucial to living the full life that Jesus said he wanted to give us (John 10:10). Conforming to a system only hampers and dulls the vivid, brilliant life that God created us to experience.

Different

Aug 15th, 2004

You know…it's just very interesting that I am so…different.

Everything about me is usually the opposite of everyone else, or at least the opposite from what I am "supposed" to be.

We were at a men's retreat this weekend (Yes, all 5 of us! Therein lies the first oddity) and I just thought, this is *SO* not me. I am not a "man's man". I am not like these guys. I don't have anything to discuss with them, and it was accentuated because they were at a manly thing for men.

I am all fine with being a man and stuff…there are plenty of ways that I am "manly". But somehow that particular homogenous group made me notice again how different I am.

And most of the time I am OK with that, but there are definitely times that I notice it more, and wish I was not always *SO* different. Not that I want to be like everyone else—I don't think I ever have wanted that, or that it is even a potential emotion for me. More just weariness of always being *so* different.

But in the end, I think that is the beauty of God's creation. No matter how many labels we make, no matter how many groups, classifications, organizations, cliques, brandings, etc, etc, etc. that we make, we are ALL unique. Every last one of us. We try to fit in (most of us) because it somehow makes us feel like we belong. But really in the end, we are all completely unique. And that's a great thing!

There are those of us who are so weird that we can't help but be noticeably different. (Like me!) And there are some who blend in a bit better, but really, we are all different.

There is amazing depth to that. We are created in the image of God, so how can we all be so different? What does that possibly say about the character, personality, and "uniqueness" of God? Might it say that he is a might bit more vast and varied and not-pin-down-able than we like to categorize him as being? Perhaps…

All I am saying is, sometimes I grow weary of being "different", but all I have to remember is that is exactly who God made me to be and there is Joy in that. There is jaw-dropping joy. The sheer immensity of his creativity is mind-boggling.

I am creative like my Creator. I am also quite willing to think outside of the box—again, like my Creator. Today, it's just good to remember that God uses my weirdness to reveal his kingdom around me. So long as my focus is on him, he will be right there with me, applauding my weirdness.

Yours too! So go on…be weird!

The Unexpected

Oct 8th, 2004

Just wanted to honor a friend tonight.

Recently I offended a friend. My openness and forthrightness and opinion sharing can sometimes cross invisible boundaries without knowing it. Such is never my intention. The only boundaries I want to cross are comfort-zone borders, which tend to keep people from thinking or growing, or even keep us in negative patterns of behavior.

But I never want to use my words to intentionally harm people.

That said, with my best intentions at heart, I still hurt a friend.

Now, what happens when you hurt someone? If it's in the heat of the moment, often you will get hurt back! A quick verbal reaction to your perceived verbal attack is a good first maneuver in hand-to-hand verbal combat.

Or, sometimes the recipient of the initial verbal lashing will be so hurt that nothing comes out…or perhaps the moment was so fast there was no time to react. However it happens, the feelings of hurt are allowed to fester, and to grow, and to morph into feelings of anger, bitterness, contempt, and eventually hatred.

All of that over what might just have been a misunderstanding.

I think the words that hurt my friend may have been more than a misunderstanding. We see something that my friend holds very dear from very different angles, and there's nothing wrong with that, until in my not so subtle ways, I speak so strongly *for* my opinion that it inherently attacks my friend's deeply held opposing opinion.

Even with that, my friend was able to do the unexpected.

The very next time we were together, there was no lingering awkwardness. There was no bitterness, no pretending nothing was wrong. There was just a frank, open, real confrontation of the issue. A crushing blow was not met by a return crushing blow, but a two-way, let's understand what happened conversation.

I think that's how it's supposed to be, and yet, after it happened, I realized that it was totally unexpected. Not what would normally happen.

So many of us are relationally unhealthy, that we would bottle it up, or fight fire with fire, and blast our loose-tongued friend for the hurt they have inflicted upon us.

But open, honest relationships need to always be that. Open and honest. Only in that can there be true friendship and freedom.

Very cool.

So, do the unexpected. Live a little like Jesus. Go out on a limb. You will amaze the target of your kindness and perhaps God will do something unexpected in you.

Forgiveness

You know, I guess I always assume God's forgiveness. There are so many stories telling me how ready God is to forgive me. He's just waiting for me to come back. And I completely believe it. I just forget how much it costs.

I was noticing recently that it is not easy to forgive.

That sounds silly, even as I write it. You'd think by age 30, I could understand that it is hard to swallow hurt and forgive someone.

But I guess I don't.

Sometimes it is easy for me. Sometimes the hurt is not so deep, the loss is not so great, and the forgiveness can be dished out a bit easier.

But sometimes it isn't easy. Sometimes the hurt does run deep. Sometimes the foundation of trust has been slowly eroded for so long that it feels like it is beginning to crumble.

And I wondered, how does He do it? How does he forgive me over and over and OVER again. I must hurt him so much. But his love surpasses the boundaries of my wildest imagination. That much is quite obvious.

Father, help me to live in your love so much today that I can see past all my hurt and love the people around me like you do. I can't understand all the hurt from *me* that you have eaten, that you've forgotten over the years. And I am sure there will be lots more. But I think you can help me. Please do. There is no greater gift I can give anyone than even a shadow of your love.

Let your love flow through me now.

<u>Your Love Living</u>
(2004)

chorus
> Let your love flow through me now
> So everyone will see

How their Father loves them
    And may my life forever be
A reflection of your love living in me

I once was lost, but now I'm found
    Those words, they echo through my brain
Cause I know the sum, the full amount
    Of what my life was when you came

Oh, I know…I'm not alone
    There are so many like me
Broken and empty, their pain unknown
    Let them know your love in me

Living…and breathing
    A warm touch from You
Broken…and needing
    The Friend I've found in You
    Let your love flow through

—Words and Music by Greg Campbell.

It's Not About Me

Jan 27th, 2005

New book on the shelf (from our amazing Library system...any book I want.. FOR FREE! Amazing!)

It's Not About Me—by Max Lucado

I read the first couple chapters this morning. He is a great writer. Simple, engaging, says things in a way that makes you want to think about them more.

I think he's right. In fact, when we saw this book, Jen and I looked at each other astonished because for a few years now, I have been discovering this truth at the heart of many life issues and have said I hope to write a book about it someday. Even by that title!!!

Max beat me to it!

So, not to fear, I have another title in mind, and actually my book is slightly different. Max seems to be heading in the primary direction of that phrase, it's not about me, it's all about HIM. The first part of the Greatest Commandment, as it is called, is to "Love the Lord your God with all your heart, soul, mind and strength." And there are many other scriptures that along with our very inner being proclaim the supremacy of God. He is all in all. Life is definitely all about Him.

But, the other part of that commandment is more what I want to focus on. So often our me-ness messes up life. First it should be about him, not us. Then, Jesus said, "Love your neighbor as yourself." After God, our attention should rest on the others around us. Not on us. See, there are lots of other scriptures that let us in on this secret.

Are you ready?

God loves you.

How about that? The all-powerful creator of the universe King...he loves you. So much that he would risk his life for you. Wait, he *did*...and he lost it...for you. In Romans, it says, "If God is for us, who can be against us?", and those words should echo through your life as a foundation for everything you do. Our every action and reaction in life.

I don't have to worry about me, because God has my back. Completely. So, my focus can be on knowing him first, and *then* on loving everyone he puts around me. Not worrying about my own life (because He does), but having genuine concern and compassion, and yes, even…JOY from serving other people around me. Letting them go first in line, and not demanding my rights or needing to speak my mind. Giving my last (insert your favorite thing here) to the person next to me instead of sneaking in the other room to make sure that I get it, and *not* them. Holding a door open for someone, shoveling mountains of snow off the sidewalk, even if you don't plan to use it.

There are so many ways to put other people first. It's a key to God's kingdom. Life would be better if we would. So, let's.

The Ugliness of Arrogance

Dec 14th, 2004

"Do justly, love mercy, walk humbly with your God…"

A line from a Steven Curtis Chapman song (one of my favorite songwriters!) Taken from a line in Micah (6:8). And really is at the core of how we are made to live.

It is not like God to be boastful or proud. Even though he has the right to be. Jesus did not come and make everyone fall to the ground with their face in the dirt…he was born in a dirty barn. As a helpless little baby. The King of the universe was wearing diapers. (From Wal-Mart probably, since they didn't have much money…)

Jesus said, "Come to me, you who are weary…I will give you rest…because I am humble and gentle…" God's very nature is the opposite of arrogant.

And for the most part, we convince ourselves we are not arrogant. We don't go around brashly proclaiming our strong points and accomplishments. We don't taunt other people with our greatness. (Well, most of us don't…) But are there other forms of arrogance?

One of my son's favorite things to do (it seems) is to let everyone know that he has seen it, heard it, done it, known it. Whatever "it" is…he's been there. And, for the most part, he's completely right. He has experienced all of those things. So it's been frustrating trying to understand why it rubs Jen and I the wrong way when he says those things, even when he is right.

Well, for some reason last night, I saw it. It is arrogance. It is the pride of being better than someone else. Or, at least not bested by another's accomplishments or experiences. Don't we see this all the time? We have run into quite a few folks along our path who *always* know something about everything…and need to let you know that. Perhaps they don't really, but you're still going to hear a little information, a story, or something about any topic you bring up.

There are actually several proverbs that mention the fact that it is often better to *not* say anything. I think that's because part of who we are is wanting to be in the know. Not left out. On the inside. And so in our arrogance, we display our accomplishments. It may not seem that way, or even be our main intent…but it comes across that way, and, I think you'll agree, rubs folks the wrong way. Perhaps just a little, but there's still some rubbin' goin' on.

So we were trying to teach Ian last night in a brief moment of openness that Jesus was completely humble and gentle. He did not need to be right, or the best, or even keep up with the best. He just loved mercy, did justly, and walked humbly with his God.

What a place this would be if we could follow his example!!

"Do nothing out of selfish ambition or vain conceit, but in humility consider others better than yourselves. Each of you should look not only to your own interests, but also to the interests of others."—Philippians 2:3-4 NIV

"No, O people, the LORD has already told you what is good, and this is what he requires: to do what is right, to love mercy, and to walk humbly with your God."—Micah 6:8

"The most important commandment is this: 'Hear, O Israel! The Lord our God is the one and only Lord. And you must love the Lord your God with all your heart, all your soul, all your mind, and all your strength.' The second is equally important: 'Love your neighbor as yourself.' No other commandment is greater than these."—Mark 12:29-31

The God Of The Familiar

January 27th, 2004

I was just reading a bit from the New Living Translation, preparing for an upcoming worship service, and I happened to flip back to the beginning of the book, where there was a note from the publishers. They were attempting to make it clear that much effort had gone into making this translation accurate, as well as understandable to the modern reader—equally clear now as it was when it was written. They also said they translated entire thoughts rather than word-for-word, which I thought was actually a better translation technique. Some feel that you must translate word-for-word in order to be truly accurate, but that's not the way I would translate a Spanish document to English. I would use similar words (or phrases) to communicate what the speaker/writer was trying to communicate. We have phrases that mean something entirely different from the actual words…and so do the Greek and Hebrew languages.

As I read that, it made perfect sense to me. I rarely use even my former translation of choice, the NIV, anymore. As I read it, the words just have a stiff, religious feel to them—though it was quite a step into the modern world from the King James Version. My preferred translation currently is the New Living Translation…but I also use, The Message, the Contemporary English Version, and any other modern-language translation I can get my hands on. Some would say that I am reading watered-down Scripture—or just flat out deny that it is even Scripture! An older pastor friend of mine was recently joking with me about my choice of translation…how he wasn't sure if I was really a Christian, reading that sort of thing…

But you see, the thing is, we are just much more comfortable with the familiar. There are some people who still think that the King James is the best text just because it was the first English translation. (Some think that the King James was *THE* original text! Though most scholars agree, it was actually first written in Greek, Hebrew and Aramaic.) The reason there are so many strong disagreements in churches is that people long to cling to the familiar…in some ways, elevating the familiar to god-status—that it is supreme and constant, and deserving of our staunchest efforts to preserve it.

The god of the familiar is seen in what translation we can use, what seats we sit in on Sunday morning, what music is acceptable, what apparel may be worn when, and all of the things that get rigidly passed down only to preserve the sense of familiarity.

In fact, God is "the same yesterday, today and forever" but, he is not rigid. He is not mundane. He is familiar in character, but not always in method. He is a living being with a personality! Able to be different in certain instances while his core remains the rock-solid constant that he is.

He is in fact quite adaptable. He is quite personal. He knows how to speak to and love each of us—personally. He does not speak in King James to me. Sorry.

SO, next time you are tempted to stick up for something just because "that's the way we've always done it"…just remember that God changes his methods along the way too…and He's not really looking for people to follow a certain way of doing things—but for people who will follow Him on The Way.

Purity of Life

Sep 18th, 2004

I feel like I have been playing lots of games lately.

Games with our finances, making all of the right moves to extend our money and purchasing power as far as it will go. Scheduling life so that money at least will potentially continue to flow in. (Though in our circumstance, that's pretty much up to God.)

Games with our church. Trying to fit in, playing by the rules, bending the rules, back and forth, give and take.

Playing games with friends and family. Not so much me playing the games, more like watching close friends and family play various roles or games with us or each other or their own families. Relationships are a prime playground for games.

Games with my schedule. Trying to balance this and that, pretending I can do everything I have scheduled.

Games with religion. Which rules does God want us to keep, and which are just rules that we have imposed on ourselves, that only serve to restrict us from the life to the full that Jesus wants for us? Still trying to figure out what sin really is, and how we treat "sinners". Just what level of participation in our Christian games like worship, and other christian service should be permitted to them?

And in the middle of all that, I lost myself in a moment with my amazing little girl. She just smiled the most pure smile of "I-Love-Dad" that I have yet seen. And then she reached tenderly to touch my face that was 6 inches from hers.

And that's when I realized… *THAT* is life. Not any of the stuff I had been pre-occupying my brain with. Not any of the stuff I have spent 20 hours a day working on this week.

Life is the love of my daughter. Life is the laugh of my son. Life is the precious moments of seeing the hearts of my kids. Life is a moment of nothingness with my wife and best friend of 14 years. (Wife of about 7, best friend of about 14.)

The games take front stage for a majority of our time, but perhaps we can learn from the glimpses of real life we get every so often?

I'm going to try.

SECTION 3

What Is Sin?

Dentist Visit

February 2nd, 2004

I went to the dentist today. And I had a cavity drilled out and fixed. My mouth still hurts from the huge needles inserted in my gums so that I wouldn't feel any pain. (Does that sentence sound funny to you, too?) But, I am completely fixed now (no cavities) and thanks to a cool lesson from the dentist on how my mouth works, and how to take care of it (I mean a very cool in-depth lesson) I shouldn't ever have cavities again!

But, I will. I know I will. I know that I can avoid all the pain (and expense!) of the dentist now because I have been shown exactly what causes cavities, and I have experienced how much they hurt. So, all I have to do is avoid eating those certain types of foods, and continue with a good regimen of brushing and flossing.

But I won't. I will continue to make excuses to not brush, or floss. It takes too much time. I am too tired. And, I can't *really* stop eating ice cream, now, can I? It's just who I am!

Sound familiar?

Just had a conversation today with Ian about disobedience. I asked him what good he gets out of disobeying, or going against anything we have told him. And he said, well, nothing really. In today's example, he just got to stay up instead of sleeping, as Mom had told him. Then we figured out that the bad is far worse. He gets privileges removed and a strained relationship with Mom and Dad. That is very bad stuff for Ian. So, all he has to do is obey and do what he knows is right, and life will be great!

But he won't. Just like I won't.

"All of us have strayed away like sheep. We have left God's paths to follow our own. Yet the LORD laid on him the guilt and sins of us all." (Isaiah 53:6)

We are not smart. We continue to do the stuff that hurts us for what we think at the moment is our gain. Really, we just get to not take our nap (which isn't good for us anyway). Or, we get to taste the ice cream—and then have a large man jam a needle into our head and then drill half of our tooth away. Ouch!

I ended our conversation by asking Ian how his disobeying affects how much I love him. "Does it make me love you less?", I asked? "Yes…" he replied ashamedly. I firmly and lovingly assured him, "NO. You can never change that. Ever. I will always love you. You may strain our relationship by disobedience…but, I will ALWAYS love you."

I may mess up, and my relationship with my Father may need work occasionally, but I can always count on his love. He took my guilt and put it on Jesus so I would always know I can come back to him.

Rotten teeth and all.

What is sin?

April 29th, 2004, and May, 1st 2004

Whoa. That just *looks* heavy. I don't really intend for it to be. I have been think-ing about grace and sin and righteousness a bunch recently...and had some inter-esting thoughts to share, and perhaps even get some feedback from you the reader.

A friend of mine is dealing with some sin in his life—some real and acknowl-edged...and some hard to pin down. (Like, is it really sin, or not?—more on this below). And it has really made me think about what we DO with sin.

Sin is obviously anything contrary to who God is and what He wants for us. And sin is what Jesus came to pay the price for. We owed a huge, unpayable debt for our sin, and Jesus died once for all to pay for it. All of it. Forever. That is grace. Grace gives us freedom to live, as messed up as we are, in the fullness of God's love and presence and greatness. Knowing full well that our freedom has been bought—*past tense*—and that we <u>are</u> God's Righteousness. (2 Corinthians 5:21) It does not depend on what we *do*. That is awesome. That is incredible. That is what we need to remember when we are worried about losing favor with God. Righteousness is not *EARNED* (even though we may convince ourselves that it can be), rather, it is the free gift of God, so that no one can boast. (Eph 2:8-9)

But, what do we *DO* with sin? How do we *live out* righteousness? Better yet, how do we help each OTHER live out righteousness? Do we? Should we?

See, when I was at Bible college, I remember a big emphasis on accountability groups and how they are vital to your "walk" as a Christian. I have always been kinda leery of them. Never been a part of one (officially, at least...) because it seems to be so driven by the whole guilt thing to me. It's righteousness motivated by Do-s and Don't-s and the guilt of having to report your failings to your closest friends. I don't think that is what Jesus was all about.

A friend of mine recently told me that Jesus was all about making people con-form. I said quite the opposite. There's no "make" in Jesus. He does not guilt people into things. He does not condemn the broken. The only folks he railed on were the "Religious Right" of the day. The keepers of the Rules. The Pharisees. And was he bashing their sin? No. Actually he was bashing their attempt at righteousness! How crazy is that?

From my reading of his life, and from my living daily with him now, it seems to me that Jesus is not about holding me to a sheet of rules or keeping track of my every move and grading each step I take. Jesus *is* about the full life of righteousness in him and in his grace.

Isn't he?

Why then do we try *so hard* not to sin? This is where it gets fuzzy. And what is sin? Do we keep the extra stringent rules that Jesus told the Jews? He said that murder is not just killing someone, it's your anger toward them too. And adultery is not just sleeping with someone, it's your lustful thoughts too. Or, do we split hairs and try and argue around what each of the ten commandments really means etymologically? Do we keep all 600 or so of the laws in the old testament? Or perhaps even add some more—modern life has introduced so many new evils...Or, do we only go by the laws recorded in the New Testament?

Is sin the acting out of the evil in our heart? Like malicious words spoken in anger or bitterness, sexual deviancy in its various forms, drunkenness, stealing, murder...all attitudes of the heart brought to fruition in sinful actions. Or is sin simply the evil in our heart? Should we be convicted (in our spirit and by others) for the evil that is in our heart, even if that evil is kept in check—kept inside?

The other night, my friend, whom we shall call Javier for anonymity, asked me to stop him from eating before he gets gluttonous. We were eating a rather scrumptious meal, and he did not want to sin in his great pleasure. And I asked him, is it *really* gluttony (and thus, a sin) if we eat one bite too many? He said, "Yes...", but upon clarification, he said it's just an attitude.

I think I agree that sin is an attitude, or a condition of the heart. But I am not sure that we need to be so cautious in all that we do that we do not step one foot over the line. That we might somehow offend or lose favor with God with one bite too many. Was that Javier's motivation? I don't think so. But on the outside it appeared that way.

I don't think that is how Jesus wants us to live. Paul said in Gal 2:21, "I am not one of those who treats the grace of God as meaningless. For if we could be saved by keeping the law, then there was no need for Christ to die." Certainly a desire to "Be holy as (God is) Holy" is not treating grace as *meaningless* is it?

In the end, I think not. More on this later. There is merit to striving everyday to be more of who Jesus is. But our motivation needs to be kept in check. I don't think that God wants us doing good to earn his favor. We can't. I don't think He wants us doing good to earn the favor of others. That is missing the point. He certainly is not about to guilt us into doing what is right—or not doing what is wrong. But he does tell us how life will be best.

What do we DO with sin? How much do we have to keep in check? Perhaps we are asking the wrong questions? Perhaps we should not focus on how much sin is too much. I think the better question is, how can I live the life-to-the-full that Jesus came to give me?

THIS is eternal life...to know YOU the One True God and Jesus Christ whom You sent. (John 17:3—emphasis mine)

Know Him. Live with Him. Love Him. Jesus will continue the work He began in us. (Philippians 1:6)

Sin—in every form—is a lack of trust in God. Every one. It is saying, "God, I know better than you on this one...I'm gonna do it *MY* way!"

Think about it...

Stealing is not trusting God to provide. Fear is not trusting that God is in control. Gossip is not trusting God to work things out. Hate is the same thing—we hate, and spew forth hatred because we are trying to take matters into our own hands. If someone has wronged us, in any way, the right thing to do is to love them—the same as always—and let the Judge take care of the injustice.

Lust (and really any sexual sin, like adultery, etc) is not trusting God to meet our sexual needs in the way He designed, in marriage with one life-long partner. Murder is just an extension of anger—mentioned above. Drunkenness—again, an attempt to take matters into our own hands, which is ironic in the case of drunkenness.

Pride? Pride is kinda the same as not trusting God. It can underlie many sins. It is the sin that says I am the one in control, I am the one who made this happen, I am the reason that I am so good. Essentially, pride is saying I AM GOD. (Which is again, not trusting God with control in our lives—not submitting to Him).

So when it comes down to it, when you sin, when I sin, it's really saying "I don't completely trust You in this area, God...I think I will try my own way."

There is a way that seems right to a man, bit in the end it leads to death. *(Proverbs 14:12, 16:25)*

Trust God—Sin Less.
Hmm...that was cool.

When we trust Jesus with our lives, we get to be sinless! Trust God—Sin Less! Ha!!

God made him who had no sin to be sin for us, so that we might become the righteousness of God. *(2 Corinthians 5:21)*

For he chose us in him before the creation of the world to be holy and blameless in his sight. *(Ephesians 1:4)*

YES!!!

Perhaps it was not clear what I am talking about, with what is sin, and what do we do with it. I completely agree with the responses I have heard so far saying basically, "It's the wrong question…don't ask what is sin, do what is good, and sin will have no room in your life." I completely agree.

Now, my question is…once someone has let sin in the door, what do you do with *that*? Since, by our very nature, we are all sinners and all prone to sinful thoughts and acts and words—even though we are saved by grace, even though when we live our lives in daily connection with Jesus, we still get caught up in sin…what do we do then?

Do we have to confess every single sinful act or thought, or risk sliding deeper into sin? Do we walk in fear that we might stumble or sin? Do we hammer on people who are stuck in a sinful thought pattern that is leading them down a road that might end in sinful actions, hoping that by that correction we might save their souls from hell?

Or, do we accept God's grace and understand our brokenness and fallenness and push ahead toward the prize for which Christ Jesus called us heavenward and not languish over each and every sin to the point of despair because of our enormous guilt? Do we mete out God's grace in the form of loving, sympathetic, compassionate, understanding helpfulness to our brothers and sisters who are struggling with trusting God—and living or thinking sinfully?

Which is it? What do we *DO* with sin?

The Heart

May 3rd, 2004

The Power Of The Heart

Proverbs 4:23 says "Guard your heart, for it is the wellspring of life." We don't often say the word "wellspring"—but I think we get the general gist. The Prover-berator (is that a word?) is saying that we *are* what is in our heart. Jesus said that too. He said, "For out of the heart come evil thoughts…" (Matt 5:19) and he revisits that idea several other times. For example, "Where your treasure is, there your heart will be also." (Luke 12:34). Our heart is who we are and affects us more than we tend to give it credit for.

We like to pretend to be logical, smart, planning, thinking, and got-it-together sort of folks. We study scripture, we know what we're supposed to do, how we're supposed to live, and we are good at it. To a point. For a while. But then, things get a bit twisted. We start to have discussions with ourselves. What we thought we knew, we begin to question. We begin to rationalize, and excuse. And before you know it, our heart has picked us up and dragged us away. To a place we did not want to be (or think it possible that we would be).

None of us is too far from that place. The place of irrationality. The place of emotional reasoning that is contrary to where God wants us to be. We are sinners. Every last one of us. The Bible tells me so. (Romans 3:23) (If you meet someone who thinks they are not, they are mighty confused. Their heart has a good grip on them.) Each one of us can be easily tricked, easily led by our heart to a place we do not want to go. Remember that the next time you are looking down on someone (especially a Christian brother/sister) for their poor choices.

Jesus mentioned that as well when he said, "Why do you look at the speck of sawdust in your brother's eye and pay no attention to the plank in your own eye?" (Matthew 7:3) He says in another place, "…first take the plank out of your eye, and then you will see clearly to remove the speck from your brother's eye." (Luke 6:42) He does not say we should not help each other when we see someone caught up by their heart. He says, don't forget about *YOUR* heart problem.

Dealing With Heart Problems

So what do we do with this? What shall we do with our heart that carries us off and so easily tricks us? How can we be saved? Actually, Paul used those very words in Romans 7, one of my favorite pictures of God's grace working in a Jesus follower's life. "Who will rescue me from this body of death? Thanks be to God—through Jesus Christ our Lord!" (Romans 7:24-25) He was lamenting the war that is constantly raging inside of him, doing what he doesn't want to and not doing what he wants to. And the conclusion is, "I am *so* glad I don't have to worry about it!!!" God's grace is the answer. His grace is sufficient!

So, what…do we just go on sinning, living whichever way we want? "There is a way that seems right to a man, but in the end it leads to death." (Proverbs 14:12, 16:25) The Proverberator (I think I like that…) thought that was so important, he said it twice! We may convince ourselves (or rather, be convinced by our hearts) that we are OK, and proceeding in an OK direction. But God says if you go off the path of what I say is best, it only leads to death. I am of the opinion that God's grace covers our eternal soul in this case, as there is no sin that Jesus death did not cover (Hebrews 7:27 and many more in Hebrews) but there is wisdom and life in living the way God has laid out for us.

"I run in the path of your commands, for you have set my heart free" (Psalm 119:32)

"Blessed is the man…(whose) delight is in the law of the Lord…Whatever he does prospers." (Psalm 1:1-3)

"But small is the gate and narrow the road that leads to life, and only a few find it." (Matthew 7:14)

The Narrow Road

Ahh, the "Narrow Road". Oft used to proclaim Christianity's hold on the stairway to heaven, but not necessarily dealing strictly with salvation. It is quite clear in scripture (including ones I have already mentioned here) that Jesus is God's sacrifice for *everyone's* sin. So, he is *the only* way to be reconciled to God. But so often we focus on the eternal nature of salvation and not the current and daily aspect of it. Jesus said, "I have come that they may have life, and have it to the full." (John 10:10) And elsewhere it says, "And this is eternal life, to know you the One True God and Jesus Christ whom You sent." (John 17:3) We talk about Christianity as a relationship, not a religion, but I think we too often treat it as the latter. Daily working our way to a favorable standing with God. Trying hard to achieve righteousness on our own. Thinking that perhaps if we give a little extra effort, that just may be possible. Paul said, "If righteousness could be gained through the law, then Christ died for nothing!" (Galatians 2:21) We are all aware of that salvifically (ooooo...big seminary word from the Bible College grad!!! Means, regarding eternal salvation.) But, we do not live it in our daily lives. We strive for a perfection that is not attainable.

And, unfortunately, some of us hold others to that unattainable goal as well.

The Path Runner

Look at the Psalms quoted above again. One of my favorite pictures in scripture is Psalm 119:32. I *run* in the path of your commands, for you have set my heart free! My picture is of a man in those short runners shorts and a tank top with the racer's number plastered on his chest and on his back. (So, *lots* of skin showing.) Water bottle in hand, sometimes refreshing his dry throat, sometimes refreshing his sweaty face. And on either side of him, a HUGE wall of thorn bushes. Nasty, prickly, and completely dominating his view on every side...except straight ahead.

The path is smooth and easy to tread, but narrow. And immediately to either side are the thorn bushes, and where those are not, there are huge, ankle-spraining holes. And where those are not, there are venomous snakes, blending in to the surrounding dust. As his eyes remain straight ahead, he is not at all tempted to step off the path, and he just *runs* as fast as he can.

Most of the other runners have already gotten themselves tangled in the bushes, or crippled by an ankle-spraining hole, or even killed by the bite of the venomous snakes. But this guy keeps going. Looking straight ahead and running hard in the way he knows he should go.

But occasionally, his tired mind and body want to stop. They want to rest. Some of those breaks in the bushes seem navigable. "I bet, if I am careful...I could avoid that stuff," he begins to convince himself. And, funny thing is, as he keeps entertaining this thought, the holes seem to be getting less deep. Even the bushes are shrinking. But, he keeps running.

"I really am tired, and this seems like a good place to stop." He scans the almost totally clear area for a good place for a break, and thinks to himself, "I bet those stories of venomous snakes are just exaggerations misinterpreted through many fanciful stories told around campfires! I could certainly *see* them if they were really here!" And now, with almost no obstacles in sight, he steps off the path for a break.

"Wow! This feels great!" the resting runner proclaims. "What was I ever worried about?" And he continues to enjoy the rest as others pass him by on the Narrow Path. "I'll catch up to them eventually," he reassures himself.

But what he does not see, that the other passers-by see quite clearly, is that he is not sitting on the relaxing, flat, care-free ground he thinks he inhabits. He is, in fact, *right* in the middle of a thorn bush. Twisted and caught, but with a smile on his face! The Path Runners stop and ask if they can help, but there is no response from the man in the thorns. He doesn't even seem to hear them. So they continue on, asking the Path Maker to help him.

After a relaxing, restful experience, the runner begins to notice a strange itching sensation. More than an itch…almost painful. "Where is that *coming* from?" he wonders. "Why am I SO itchy?!?" As he scratches, the thorns dig deeper into his flesh. Causing more pain.

Soon, a couple Path Runners stop and ask him if they can help. "What? Help me with what?" he asks, puzzled. Then they ask him if he is aware that he is caught in a thorn bush. "WHAT!?? What are you *talking* about?" He looks around and sees the flat ground around him, and his trusty water bottle, and retorts, "Are you serious??? The thorn bushes are back there! It's flat ground right here. So, I thought it would be safe to step off the Path for a break."

The Path Runners look concerned, and they try quite intensely to convince the thorn-stuck runner that he is in fact caught in a thorn bush and in a good bit of danger. He will have none of it, and sends them on their way. They reluctantly leave, and ask the Path Maker to open the ThornDweller's eyes.

After such a strange experience as that, the runner thought it was about time to get up and catch his competition.

"What were they ON??? It's so flat here, I can't even see the PATH! Thorn bushes my…" The ground beneath his feet truly did have a homogeneous appearance, blending the path into the surrounding area. But he was pretty sure of which direction he needed to go, and he began jogging at a rapid pace to catch up to his competitors.

He ran, and ran, and ran…"Why have I not caught anyone yet? Where are they?" he pondered. And he thought of those two Path Runners who so vehemently attempted to convince him that he was stuck in a thorn bush! Their certainty perplexed him. "Where *are* those thorn bushes anyway?"

After a long time had passed of running straight ahead on the pathless ground, he came upon another group of Path Runners. They too were convinced that he was stuck in a thorn bush, and they spiced up the story a bit by revealing the presence of a venomous snake poised and ready to strike his left wrist.

"OK guys…this has gone a bit too far. I would really like it if you would all just leave me alone. *PLEASE*. I do not know *what* you are talking about. I do not see the thorns. I do not see the snake. My path looks clear to me!"

They pleaded with him, and some were angry. It was so obvious he was in trouble. Some even called the ThornDweller names. But he would not budge. He did not see any thorns, and so he finally outlasted their persistent pestering and they left him alone, asking the Path Maker to rescue him from the venomous snake.

"Were they really right?" he thought, "Am I stuck in thorns, and just can't see it? I have always been on the Narrow Path, and I am trying my best to run it now! I just can't really see it…but I know it's this way." And he turned and began again in the same direction.

All of a sudden, there was a crippling pain in his wrist. "WHAT was THAT?!!" He looked down and saw two red marks on his left wrist. "WHERE did that come from???" He winced in pain and to his amazement, he saw a venomous snake slither away in the dirt. And as he tried to tend to his wound, which throbbed with increasing pain, he began to notice other scratches on his body. "Where did those come from?" he thought.

As the painful moments passed, he began to notice even further startling appearances. All around him, thorn bushes began to crop up. Slowly at first, and then increasingly violently, as though they were actually alive! Twisting and grabbing at him and catching him up in their painful grasp. All at once, as he began to lose consciousness, he saw that he was in fact quite clearly caught in a thorn bush.

The Path Runners who saw the ThornDweller who had succumbed to the venomous snake paused for a moment to reflect on the painfully obvious fact that with only a few poorly chosen steps off of the Path, that could be them. They thanked the Path Maker for the clear Path, and for his Direction and asked him to continue to protect them from the perils along the Path.

And they continued to run—free-hearted—on the Narrow Path.

Now, I made that up. But, do you see the power of the heart? It can convince us of things that are just not true. It can blind us to things that we know are lies. It can carry us off to a place we know we should not be. Our heart can not keep us from salvation. No sin is greater than Grace. But it can choke the life out of us. And keep us from the Life the Path Maker intended.

So, please…Stay on the path.

Gardening Observation

June 24th, 2004

We planted our first garden this year! We were so excited as the winter temperatures gave way to the warmer summer air (mostly…we are in NY, ya know!) The gardening aisles began to fill up at Wal-Mart and Ian couldn't wait to grow veggies and even flowers out front!

So one Monday (our day off) I headed out at 6:30am and started digging up a patch of weeds over on the side of our yard where we would be putting our garden. It had not been touched in years but the soil underneath looked pretty good. So we dug out all the weeds and grass, turned up the soil, and planted our seeds.

We watered and waited and watered and waited…and wondered if they would grow…

THEY DID!

But, so did the weeds!!!! They came back with a *vengeance*.

And it made me think of our lives. When you take someone new to the ways of the Kingdom and they experience the new life like our garden did, it's great at first! Everything is new! But the weeds are so used to growing there, they come right back…with a vengeance! It takes time, and care and lots and lots of weeding to get the soil to the point that the good stuff can grow free of weeds.

And you know what…it's never "free" of weeds. But they do lose their footing the more time you take to tend and weed the garden. To care for it.

Just an observation from a part-time gardener.

I gotta get out there and check that soil…

They Look The Same

July 28th, 2004

I was gardening again today. To tell the truth, it's slightly addicting. It's kinda predictable, and mindless, and just different from what I do. So I slip out to check out the garden for a moment, and end up being out there doing various garden things for a half hour or more!

Well today I noticed that weeds are not only abundant, they are tricky. They actually seem to match the plants that are around them. In stature, in leaf type…it's crazy! To the point where it is so hard to tell where the weed ends and the good plant begins and vice versa. Next to the cucumber vines was a weed sprawled throughout them that was a vine and looked like a cucumber plant, until I took a closer look. Interspersed between tomato plants were tall thin leafy plants…*just like a tomato plant.*

I thought that was pretty weird.

It's just like sin. It looks just like the real thing…a lot! But it's a *weed*, bent on sucking the life out of the good plant and robbing it of all the nutrients in its soil, of the sunlight it needs, of the water it needs.

And it's worthless. The good plant produces (or is) fruit, it's food. The weed is just ugly. (Though sometimes deceptively beautiful on the outside…it's ultimately worthless.)

So be careful of the weeds in your life. Take time to examine the stuff around you and make sure they are the plants you want and not the weed look-alikes.

The Wrong One

Nov 21st, 2004

Today was our second longest day of driving ever (that I can remember). We drove 761.1 miles. That's a lot. A whole lot. But we got to see *lots* of amazing stuff along the way.

One thing we greatly anticipated on today's trip was the drive past Mt. Shasta. It is an impressive sight! Fourteen thousand plus feet of snow capped mountain towering over everything around. It is not part of a group of mountains, it's definitely the king of the hill where it stands.

Well, according to the road signs, we were still two *hundred* miles away, but we saw this cool-looking snow-capped mountain in the distance...in the direction that Mt Shasta would be...and we got excited! "Could that be it???" I couldn't really believe we could see it from so far away! It did look kinda small, but I figured that's cause of the distance.

So for 20–30 miles, we drove, in complete awe of this mountain that we could see so well from 200 miles away! We drove 50 miles, and it kept getting closer. And I became more and more convinced that it was Mt. Shasta.

Until I saw it.

On the horizon, blurred by distance and its height reduced significantly by the curvature of the earth, was an *ENORMOUS* white mountain!!! That...was the real Mt. Shasta.

And then I felt silly. I looked at what I thought had been Mt. Shasta, and then at the real thing, and I couldn't believe I had ever accepted the imposter as the real thing!!!

And that made me think. Don't we do that all the time with sin? Don't we size up our sin, convincing ourselves that it is indeed the real thing? Even though we know our Father has something far better for us in mind? We convince ourselves that the puny imitation we see is really the majestic genuine article we actually want.

But it's not.

One of Satan's grand schemes is to get us to accept a counterfeit. Often, the sins that most entangle us appear to be the thing we most need. Or, if we notice it's not quite right, we convince ourselves that it is the thing we need. But then if it is placed next to the real deal, it seems so small and worthless in comparison.

Mt. Shasta is an amazing piece of God's handiwork. Really. If you've never seen it, pictures just can't capture the jaw-dropping hugeness of this big piece of rock! It's incredible.

And to think I was willing to accept a little ant hill in comparison!

God reminded me today to watch out for counterfeits in my life. To always keep my eyes open for the *real* deal. It is so much more amazing. Boy, is that true!!!

"I Can't Believe She Did That!"

Dec 8th, 2004

I have been noticing again that we are really good at recognizing sin. Especially in others. We are so good at seeing what is wrong in our neighbor. And in a way, that's not bad. Wrong is wrong. But the problem is, we see the wrong and say, "I can't believe they did that!" when the reality is we certainly *can* believe it, because *we* do it.

I guess we Christians are the best at this. We have this sense of self-righteousness, the righteousness that we have earned by our intense effort to live out the righteousness commanded in scripture. We may not get it *all* right, but we are working hard to get most of it right.

So, when we see someone who is clearly not even trying to do what God says, then it's easy to point our finger in accusation. "I can't believe he did that!"

I think this is what has kept the church from really helping people. We work so hard to be righteous, to obey all of God's commands, either out of fear of God, or out of a genuine desire to please him, but either way, it only leads to frustration. WE CAN'T DO IT. We can never be righteous through keeping the law. That is why Jesus died on the cross. We couldn't beat sin and death. But he could. So through faith in him, we are made righteous.

We know that. We do. But it's so easy to think we are righteous by our own efforts, and condemn the others who aren't. But then we close the door on any chance to share the deep love that God has for them.

Do you remember how Jesus treated "sinners"? Who was it that Jesus hung out with, spent his time with? Was it the clean-cut, church-going, got-it-together folks? No! Not even close. Jesus spent his time with the dregs of society. The tax-collectors, the prostitutes, the lepers, the zealots, the gruff fishermen (don't know if they were the dregs…), he was even ostracized for giving attention to the children.

He spent his time with the sinners. He wasn't offended. He didn't have to wash his hands after they left. He wasn't too holy to be around them. He did not demand that they change their ways before they entered his presence.

He just loved them.

Wow, if we could do that. Instead of playing junior-high gossip and finger-pointing games…we would help a lot more people know the love God has for them, and in turn, help a lot more of them experience the joy of living a life led by the Spirit, instead of being trapped by sin.

True freedom comes in letting Jesus be our righteousness, not striving for it ourselves. That righteousness is a love for the One who is righteousness. We want to be like our Dad. Not because we're afraid of his punishment, but because we think he is the most amazing Dad ever there was.

And when we live like that, His love is the only thing that matters. We know we are loved, so opinions of others don't matter. The faults of others are not offensive, as we know we are faulty as well. Love for our neighbor is easier as we admit our righteousness is not ours, it is from God. Otherwise, we are just like them, hurting, lost, and missing the abundant life God wants for us. A life spent with him.

So next time you're pointing the finger, just remember, Jesus is not pointing fingers at you. You are loved. And so are they.

How Did I Get Here??

May 6th, 2004

Continuing on this theme of what is sin, and what does it do to us, I was reading the story of David and Bathsheba again today. (sidenote…I have always thought that she has the funniest name in light of the rest of the story…) We all know that story. What's that? You don't? Well, let me recount it to you quickly. (Well, my version of "quickly", anyway!)

Background on King David

David has spent something like 30 years as the publicly proclaimed King of Israel but hiding in caves running from the current king in power—Saul. God told Samuel to anoint David as king and then everything went downhill from there. Everything David did was successful—God was definitely with him. So, Saul was jealous and tried to kill David—several times! And David faithfully refused to play God and take matters into his own hands, though he was more powerful, and though he knew that God had already anointed him as king. He knew that was God's job, and no matter how hairy it got, he stuck to that conviction.

Scripture tells the stories of all the battles David won against God's enemies. And it says several times that David was "a man after God's own heart."

The Bathing Beauty

But then it happened. One day, after David woke up from a nap, he went out on his balcony which overlooked the city. And as he was looking around, he noticed a woman taking a bath on her roof (and The Message adds, "The woman was stunningly beautiful").

Now, David had this thing for the ladies. Really. If I remember correctly from recent readings, David already has 3 wives and in 2 Sam 5:13 it says, "David married more wives and concubines, and had many sons and daughters." Whoa!

So, he wanted more. This woman was stunningly beautiful, and he wanted her. Which, I guess by the culture he was living in would have been fine. So he asked someone to go find out who she was. The report came back that she was Bathsheba, the wife of Uriah the Hittite.

(A little more background…remember that David had been on the run for decades? During that time a band of tough guys joined forces with him (called the Mighty Men) and Uriah was one of these loyal, awesome dudes.)

Turning Point #1

This is the first turning point. A huge cavern between the period at the end of 2 Sam 11:3 and the first letter of verse 4. A moment when David could have honored God or himself. He has already set his heart in motion toward this lady. (Read more about the power of our hearts out of control in The Heart.)

What a huge bummer when he finds out she is not available. How he hoped that she would be. She would make a fine addition to his wife collection. But, she's not available. She is Uriah's wife. I will honor Uriah and God by moving on. She's not available. But…she *is*…kinda. You can hear him begin to rationalize, "She's all alone…her husband is away…she really *is* beautiful…it's just one time…it can't be that bad…can it?"

The argument perhaps raged for a good while—David has been so faithful in his life—so focused on what was right and good. Three chapters ago, God said this about David, "David reigned over all Israel and was fair to everyone." EVERYONE? Whoa. David was a really cool guy. With strong convictions, and huge faith and trust to carry them out. So there must have been a battle. Whether at this moment or previously…the battle was raging.

But then we come to verse 4, and the text reads: "Then David sent for her." There's more, but that says it all. Now, don't get me wrong, Bathsheba had to agree to come, agree to hang out, and agree to get in bed. She is quite culpable as well. But, the weight of this decision—the guilt of the sin I believe—is right here in those 5 words. When David sent for her, that is when he intended to "despise God" (as he is later accused of doing) and do what seemed right in his own eyes.

So, they have this one-night-stand kinda thing. David probably had some remorse about it, but, ya know…being king, he pretty much got away with it. He had fun with Bathsheba, and she went home…end of story. But she got pregnant. Oh my…the consequences of sin. One bad choice leads to a predicament.

David sends word to the battlefield that he wants Uriah to come home and give a report to him about the war. Uriah heeds the call and reports to David all that God is doing. After some small talk—most likely quite awkward on David's part at least—David says, "Go home and relax." All part of a pretty sneaky plan to cover his tracks.

The next day, David is quite angry to find that Uriah did not go home. He stayed in Jerusalem at the palace entrance. He did not sleep with his wife. He did not give David an easy way out.

Turning Point #2

Again, we come to a turning point. Perhaps another battle raged in the heart and mind of the Man after God's Own Heart. He even had a whole day to think about it. Uriah slept one more night at the palace entrance. He could own up to his sin, and ask forgiveness from the man he wronged. (That's BIG owning up as adultery was serious stuff in God's law, punishable by stoning for both offenders) Or, he could find another way to cover his tracks.

The next morning, David decided to go his way again and sent the command to have Uriah put at the front of the battle when he returns, and for everyone else to pull back so he would be killed. OK, HOLD ON HERE. Man After God's Own Heart??? What's going on here? What happened to the man who TWICE was in a position to kill the man (King Saul) who was hunting him and both times refused to take matters into his own hands. The same man who relented from exacting revenge on Nabal who had wronged him and his men. The same man who had so much faith that he took on a NINE-FOOT warrior with just a sling shot and some stones?

How did he get here? Uriah was sent to the front of the battle, and killed, as David had asked. And again, the commander who gave the order, the other soldiers—others have responsibility in this too—but, ultimately David killed Uriah. And for what? To cover his tracks? To get his wife? David is later confronted by a prophet named Nathan who accuses David (well, God through Nathan) of having "murdered Uriah and stolen his wife." He also says, "Why, then, have you despised the word of the LORD and done this horrible deed?"

This was not pretty. This was certainly not "after God's own heart". So what happened? How DID he get there? How do we? How do we go so far that men who dedicate their lives to serving God are accused in the dozens of molesting little boys? That people in positions of trust are guilty of violating that trust to the point of rape and murder?

One Small Step for Mankind, One Giant Leap for Sin

Sin is progressive. We are sinful by nature. David said in Psalm 51 after his eyes were opened to the sheer ugliness of what he had done, "I was born a sinner". He's right. It is our nature. To choose for our self. To go against God's wisdom.

And usually it starts small. A stray thought. A prideful moment. A bending of the line.

Often there is a battle, even a fierce battle at times. But often we shield ourselves from it and press on down the path we should not be on. One little step after another leads to bigger ones. Sometimes to cover our guilt or shame. Sometimes because we had fun. Sometimes because we didn't get caught. Whatever the reason, it starts to snowball.

And before you know it, we have killed a man and "taken (his) wife to be (our) own."

A Broken and Repentant Heart...

Do you find yourself asking, "How did I get here?" I just read an old journal entry today, and I was writing about stuff that I have been dealing with for years. Ways of thinking that are contrary to God's heart. And I said those very words. "How did I get here again?" My heart still belonged to God, but it had fallen in a pool of mud and needed some serious cleaning.

Thankfully, that is what God does. I love the line in the story where after David confesses his sin ("I have sinned against the LORD") Nathan says to him, "Yes, but the LORD has *already* forgiven you." I think that is SO COOL! David needed to surrender the fight to do what he wanted to do, but not *IN ORDER* to receive forgiveness! It was to clean his heart—to make the relationship right.

We *so often* live with the guilt-driven idea of confession being a necessary thing to receive God's forgiveness. The idea of making a list, checking it twice—and divulging our every evil to our Maker. We do this expecting that he will forgive. But, we also do it *so that* he will. I think this line from Nathan more accurately reflects the heart of God.

Jesus said the words, "It is finished", and everything changed. Before that, God could choose to forgive looking forward to the cross which covered the sins of everyone. But now we have the assurance of forgiveness. Always. Not a forgiveness that comes each time we offer a sacrifice for each blunder committed. Not a forgiveness for some sins, but withheld for others more heinous (or more plentiful). A total and complete forgiveness. "A Broken and repentant heart, O God, you will not despise."

When we are at a spot where we start asking, "How did I get HERE?", we have made bad choices. We are in a bad spot. But there is hope. As we admit our bad choices, and seek to restore our relationship with Jesus, he is there waiting for us. It is several steps, small but persistent to get to where we ask "How did I get here?", but a simple 180-degree turn gets us back to a right relationship with Jesus.

That, my friends, is amazing.

And equally begs the question, in a completely opposite kinda way…"How did I get here???"

SECTION 4

The LORD Gave and the LORD Has Taken Away

Loss

Nov 11th, 2004

"I came naked from my mother's womb,
and I will be stripped of everything when I die.
The LORD gave me everything I had,
and the LORD has taken it away.
Praise the name of the LORD!" (Job 1:21)

Those were the first words—words of worship—immediately following Job's hearing the news that his children had been killed in a horrible accident. And just before that he had lost much of the wealth of possessions that God had blessed him with. An amazing reaction to an extraordinary circumstance. His first thought was to worship the God who had given him life, even in the midst of the demise of the life he had known.

There is a song by songwriter Matt Redman called *Blessed Be Your Name*. It echoes those lines Job spoke so many years ago,

"You give and take away, you give and take away,
My heart will choose to say, Lord blessed be your name!"

Those words reverberated loudly—even confidently—through my head as we learned that the child for whom we had been eagerly preparing a space in our family, had stopped developing inside Mom's womb.

"You give and take away…You give and take away…
My heart will choose to say…Lord, blessed be Your name."

The first moments were just hard. Shocking. Deep sadness. Life hoped for, now lost. And this was not the first time we faced this.

About one week into our tour, there was such a shocking occurrence that we thought we had lost the baby. That was on our anniversary. Not the way we wanted to end the day. The drive to the hospital was a little over an hour. Of silence. Of doubting. Of wondering. Of self-pummeling. I felt completely culpable for the loss of this baby's life. Our lifestyle, my missed chances at reminding Jen to rest, my busyness keeping me from helping Jen with the other three kids. All things were pointing to me being the reason we had lost the baby.

But God was beyond gracious.

When we arrived at the hospital, we were greeted by a friendly nurse who was fairly convinced that the baby was doing just fine. The doctor who followed happened to be at the church we had led in worship the morning prior, and he echoed those sentiments, but they needed to do an ultrasound to make sure.

My heart skipped a beat or two in astonished joy. My soul gasped for air! I can't describe the feeling of life from death. How the Father must have felt when his son was given breath again! Even knowing the plan ahead of time, his heart must have exploded with joy knowing that not only his son, but all of us who trust in him were given back to him that day!

We went from that place, with images of a dancing baby in our head, and the hope that through a rough 6 or 7 months ahead we would emerge with a miracle baby from God.

"You give and take away…"

Yesterday, following the weekend of God giving wildly to us through his people, we experienced the pain of loss again.

Jen had been experiencing signs of trouble again (we thought) and so we went to the doctor, who put the monitor on Jen's belly to listen for the heart beat. After about 10 awkward seconds, she said, "Sometimes it's difficult to find the heartbeat with that machine."

That had not been our experience, and so we were already thinking the worst.

She turned on the ultrasound equipment, and we began looking at the baby inside. It had grown since the first time we had seen it, but it was lifeless. No movement. No heartbeat. No life.

No words were said for a time, until the doctor broke the silence, "I'm afraid I have some very bad news…"

My heart sank. It was quite final. The baby was gone. Again.

But this time, the words to that song kept replaying in my head. "You give and take away…my heart will choose to say, Lord, blessed be your name…"

And I meant it. Though I was not necessarily comforted by it just yet. We discussed the next steps and headed out to the van to go home. The song continued in my head.

When we got to the van, we just sat there in silence. We were both attempting to understand what was happening. To process it. Why would God want to give us a baby for 12 weeks, and then take it home? There were tears. There was silence. We prayed together. We talked. But the most amazing thing was happening inside my head and heart.

Instead of sadness, there was supreme confidence in God's love for me. More than just confidence, there was palpable reality. Almost like his hands on my shoulders.

And the song would not leave.

I knew the scripture was from Job, so I looked it up on the computer we had brought with us.

The first thing that stuck out to me was in the NIV translation: "Job got up, tore his robe and shaved his head, then he fell to the ground in worship." His first response was a brief moment of agony and mourning, and then he worshipped. Instead of blaming God for letting this happen, he was compelled to worship him.

That's where I lost it.

I was too! That's what I had been feeling the whole time in silence. Strong images and feelings of God's love and provision for me, for us, were present in my head. I was not consciously thinking of them. They were just there. I was not dwelling on the loss, but rather on things gained from the Giver of all good things.

And that's exactly what Job experienced.

God's bigness, his caring, his individual attention to my life, his unfathomable love—all of that had never been so near to me, so palpable, so *real*.

Words do not do the experience justice, but I really wanted to try. I was astounded by the love God has for, and was showing to *me*. I was crying, not out of sadness at our loss as much as out of overwhelming joy and gladness at my Father who loves me.

In a moment, literally less than a second, God also gave me a strong series of images that reminded me of his goodness.

There were three sets of two images. First was the hospital back in Arkansas. Image one was the deep sadness of losing the baby, and image two was the unspeakable joy of getting that life back! Second was from the weekend just past, where image one was the empty bank account and actually having zero cash being

3000 miles from home with many big bills to pay, and me asking God in a parking lot, "God, what are you going to do??". The second image connected to that was of the generosity of our Father through his people this weekend, we were given nearly $2000 by people and places that wouldn't normally be a source of such abundance. The third image was our present circumstance, the final loss of our baby, and attached to that image was a future provision from God that would blow us away with greatness as much as this loss had brought us low.

I had a very specific image, but as I am not claiming to be a prophet, I will guard that image in my heart and will let you know if that does indeed come to fruition. I don't think God gave me those images for you…but I *know* he gave them for me.

In less than a second, all of that imagery of God's attention to our lives came into focus, and I was full-on reminded of his incredible provision and love.

And again, I was brought to tears…not of sadness, but pure, unthinkable joy!

Our God is so good. So, so good.

We are sad, and still dealing with loss. Loss costs us. We won't know this member of our family until heaven. I see images of families with kids, or even our kids, and I miss the face of the baby we lost. We are definitely hurting.

But there is over all of that, a far greater peace and hope. God made me *so* aware of his presence and love in my life today, right now. He is so good that way. And I am not alone in that experience. Which makes it even cooler. Friends today have shared a similar experience, and I believe the reason Job reacted when he did was that God was as overwhelmingly present for him that day as he was for me. And Job's loss exceeds mine by such a volume as I can't imagine.

He is so good. Today, yesterday, forever.

The Lord gave, and the Lord has taken away. Praise the name of the Lord.

Outpouring

Nov 13th, 2004

We hear the word outpouring used sometimes. Well, perhaps we who are Christians even more. An outpouring of God's Spirit, or an outpouring of God's love.

I believe we have been experiencing an outpouring.

Since we received the news of the death of our baby-to-be, and since we have sent out an e-mail to family and friends, we have been the recipients of an outpouring. E-mails have come in by the dozen. Some sharing the sorrow of this life lost to us, and some sharing the joy of this life brought home to heaven. But the most notable to me is the number of emails we have received from people we even know fairly well sharing that they too have experienced similar hurt. Some even multiple times.

That just amazes me.

It is amazing that it happens. How can so many of our friends, and others, have gone through this as well. We have experienced 3 healthy pregnancies, so it seemed so improbable that we would be sitting here talking about one from our family in heaven.

But it does. A lot.

But equally amazing is the way that those folks shared with us on a deeper level the sorrow we are facing. They know the hurt. They have lived it. Almost like my experience with the story from Job's life just a few days ago. Their shared sentiments with us have also created another level of shared life that we didn't understand before.

Tragedy is a strange thing. It is tragic, yet it bring people closer. There is loss, yet there is nearly always gain. The New Testament writers speak often of trials and suffering as a blessing rather than a curse.

Fascinating.

We are living the blessing now as we thank God for bringing Jen through all of the medical procedures with full health, and as we celebrate the family he has given us here to share life with.

He is good.

There remain moments of sadness. When I see the photos of recent weeks, I remember how we were trying everything we could to help this baby survive, but in fact, baby had already gone home. I see the prenatal vitamins and remember to remind Jen to take it, then the emptiness returns. And when I brought the van around to pick up Jen at the hospital, my heart ached because it was all wrong. We were supposed to come home with a baby, not leave the baby there.

There are definitely sad times. But overwhelmingly there is hope and peace. God leads us on. We follow with joy. And hope. And trust.

"My heart will choose to say, Lord blessed be your name…"

The REST...of The Story...

Nov 15th, 2004

I am quite emotional these days.

Whether it's from the hurt of losing a baby so hoped for, or the overwhelming reality of God's love and care for *me*, or the joy of being part of the family God has given me...all of these things have brought tears to my eyes on several occasions over the past several days.

Today, I was overwhelmed again.

Some of you reading this may know the situation with our health insurance, but for the benefit of those who do not, I will summarize here briefly.

In May of this year, we received a bill for $0.00 from our health insurance provider. I thought that odd, so I called in and verified that amount. Indeed, we were paid through July. So, the subsequent month's bill was also for $0.00. The following month was slightly paid, so our bill was only about half. We paid that in a quite timely fashion.

Then, unbeknownst to us at the time, we did not receive a bill for either August or September. We were made aware of that when we received a bill for 3 months worth of premium due *immediately* in early October. Well, obviously I called and tried to figure out what was going on there. We arranged a payment plan to satisfy our insurer that we could financially bear.

Problem solved. Or, so I thought...

We were alerted to an issue with insurance when we were at the hospital in Arkansas. I told them I was aware of it, and it should be just fine. Then when we got to the doctor (where we found out we had lost our baby) we were told that our account was canceled! That was quite a shock, but I figured with a little investigation, we'd have no issue.

Boy, was I wrong!

Our bank had mailed the payment (as they have all year) by Oct 26. Plenty of time to get to our insurer. Apparently, it did not arrive. The check had not been cashed, said my bank. So, we arranged to send out another payment. In the mean time, the insurer was like a stone wall saying there was no way that our account could *ever* be reinstated. Thank you. Good bye.

All of this was happening while Jen was in surgery.

So, it was the weekend, and I could do nothing anyway, but first thing this morning (morning on the West Coast, at least) I was trying to gain my composure so that I could talk with these folks and see if we could get someone to understand what happened here.

And now...THE REST of the story...

I called in to the bank, to verify that the money was there, then phoned the insurance company. The first person I spoke with was Kennedy. I explained the whole story to him, and he said I would have to talk with a supervisor. No problem...I expected as much.

What I didn't expect was getting the *same* supervisor who had "helped" me on Friday. She had been quite rude and harsh. I told her I had called back to speak with someone regarding this situation again, and we could try again, or she may want to get someone else. She said, "I'll get someone else..."

So, Virginia answers the phone.

I had asked God to help me be completely humble and gentle, and patient, and as rational as I could be...as anger had not worked last time.

In my calmest voice, and most humble heart I could project through telephone wires, I explained our story. I told her that all of this was on top of losing a baby. I told her we don't really have a lot of money, so insurance is obviously a helpful thing.

She listened. Really, and with compassion that I could feel through the aforementioned phone lines. But, she said that the plan we are on is *very* strict, so she could not promise anything...but she would try.

I was on hold for probably about 5 minutes. Perhaps less. During that time, I really, finally, and completely felt peace. We owe thousands of dollars in new medical bills (on top of our already enormous debt), but I had full confidence that with or without insurance, God would take care of that. And, I knew that God would take care of injustice. I told God that whatever Virginia tells me, I will accept. (Which was not my story last time I was talking to these folks!) So, since I had no part in it anymore, I had peace.

I decided to look up the proverb for today. (Proverbs has 31 chapters, so you can read a chapter per day based on the day's date) I was amazed yet again at the verse I found.

"A gentle answer turns away wrath, but a harsh word stirs up anger." (Proverbs 15:1)

A wave of emotion overcame me there, as it felt like God was confirming that I was choosing the best way. His truth was present in me. Does that sound weird? It does to me, but that's how it felt. It was real. Truth was verified. Truth was with me. That's not so weird when you remember Jesus said "I am the...Truth".

Virginia came back on the line, and I braced myself for the final verdict. Good or bad, I was going to calmly accept it and trust God with the rest. That's what I told myself, at least.

She said, "Mr. Campbell? Thanks for waiting. I just wanted to let you know that...your account has been reinstated!" You could even hear the excitement in her voice when she told me.

I was again in awe of God's provision. We shared a few more words. I explained to her a little bit of what we are doing out here. I told her to expect the account to be paid up by week's end. I could not convey strongly enough the gratitude that I felt. Which is slightly odd as I didn't really do anything to earn this treatment—it was not our fault—but it felt then like they had granted me the most favor I have received since Jesus' grace.

Really, the thing God showed me here again was that life works best when we trust him. My heart had peace before the decision. Because I trusted him. The decision to reinstate our account (which was against the better judgment of a number of others I had previously spoken with) was an overwhelming bonus to the peace of trusting our Father to take care of us.

I don't know what God was trying to teach me through this whole thing. From the Proverb I read, I thought perhaps he was giving me a very vivid example of his truth. I asked Virginia to please pass on an apology for me to the other supervisor I had spoken harshly to. I figured that part, or most of her rudeness to me was instigated by my frustration and anger errantly aimed at her.

Perhaps it is part of the continuing journey of God building our trust in Him more than anything else we could ever place our trust in? Perhaps God wanted to remind us that He is our Insurance Provider? Perhaps He wanted to give Virginia an opportunity to stretch the institutional rules to love a fellow human being? Perhaps someone else whom she had to convince?

We can not know what God is doing with the stuff that happens all around us. But we can know that he does not let hurt go to waste. He will use it to allow people to see Him more clearly (his love, his grace, his provision, his caring, his justice, his…everything!) But he does work all things together for good for those who love him.

Boy do I love Him.

I am constantly reminded, with all of the amazing stuff that he has given me, the amazing people he has surrounded me with…

What do I have but Him? None of his blessings really matter without the Blesser.

I am so glad he loves me. I am so glad he teaches me everyday more about himself and his kingdom. I hope you are walking with him today too, knowing the Way, the Truth and the Life deeply.

And now you know…the *REST* of the story.

Taking Life For Granted

Sep 21st, 2004

Got a call from my parents tonight. My Dad wanted to tell me that he totaled his vehicle. It was a bit of a running joke because of our apparent propensity for automobile accidents, but they did just want to recount the details as well.

After the call I thought, "Wow. What if it was my Mom, or another family member calling to say my Dad had been killed in a mostly head-on collision this afternoon?" What a shock that would have been.

Why? Everyone dies. Why would that be a shock? Because we expect life to continue as is. Not sure why we do that, because it never does. But for some reason we persist in our delusion. We simply expect that the things we do will for the most part remain constant. That the people we love will remain constant—or at least continue breathing.

I am experiencing that a bit (on a much different level) with the church we are working for. When we signed on a couple years ago, we were a perfect fit for what they needed and vice versa. But, they have changed rapidly in many areas (and perhaps we have not?) and I find myself asking aloud, "Do we fit here?" Life is changing so much that perhaps we do not.

Life is change. Most times that's really good. Keeps things fresh, and helps us to focus on the only One who does not change. But sometimes change can be so sudden and unexpected that it rocks your world.

We have some friends whose 16 year old son was killed in a shooting accident earlier this summer. How incredibly sad. How completely unexpected. He is not supposed to be gone. I had just been thinking about that again today.

Then got the call from my parents tonight, and thought about life without my Dad. Who would take care of my Mom? Who would I call for fatherly wisdom and insight? Who could I count on for help if money was super tight? Who would I disagree with on most everything in life? Who would do my home improvement projects for me?!?? (For more on that, read *Home Handy Repairman Jack*)

I know the answer to all of those above. Romans 8:28 says, "And we know that God causes everything to work together for the good of those who love God." So, I know he would.

But, for now, I'm glad you're still with us, Dad.

Life Is SO Fragile

Aug 7th, 2004

Sixteen years old. Strong. Energetic (well, mostly...he is a teen-ager!). Parents who love him, a baby sister who might admit to that, family and friends. Life is full of potential and goodness, despite anything that might try to dampen that, life is good.

And then it ends.

Some friends of ours just lost their 16-year old son to a hunting accident. He was with some friends in Alaska, visiting his Uncle, and details are not completely known as of yet, but those are not so important as the awful reality of a life cut short.

I can not imagine the pain of losing a child. I have three so far, and we are hoping for more, and I hope that God lets me see them live a great life full of loving people and serving him. To see that cut short (even knowing that the joy of being with Jesus is the alternative) has just got to be super hard.

Somehow death and severe hardship have not touched my family. Jen's brother died shortly after we were married...that is as close as I have come. God has somehow protected my family as a whole. That is cool. But maybe not?

"Consider it pure joy...when you face trials of many kinds"—James 1:2

Hard things in life *will* come, and God wants us to accept them as tools to shape us, and tools for Him to use for His Kingdom around us. And even just as a way to understand our need for, and to deepen our trust in Him.

It is also quite clear in Scripture that while it is a blessing to live a long full life here, this is not the end, and there is much more and a much better life to come. So enjoy this life to the full (John 10:10), but know that there is something much, much better. (Too many references, but Titus 1:2, 3:7)

So, I am quite saddened at hearing of the death of our friends' son. Yet, I know God will bring good from this for those who love him (Romans 8:28). And

I know that there is hope of something much better for those who are in Jesus. And this family is.

There is no certainty of our next day, or moment or even our next breath. But live life to its fullest, live it with your Creator, live it for him, and things will go well for you. No matter what it looks like on the outside.

"Now this is eternal life: to know you the One true God and Jesus Christ whom you sent."—John 17:3 (said by Jesus)

That's it. This life *will* end. We don't know when, but we do know that eternal life is knowing God and living it with him.

Let's do it.

Quiet

Nov 4th, 2004

Quiet. The aspiration of every parent.

Just a moment. Just a brief respite in an otherwise noisy maelstrom of life.

We stayed with some friends this past week who do not have kids. They were not prepared for the two little tornadoes in the form of boys that were to invade their home. Not that our boys are bad. They are not. They are some of the most self-controlled, well-behaved, kind and considerate boys I know.

But, they are boys. And they are loud.

But as I enjoyed a brief moment of solitary quiet just now, I was thankful that there is noise in our home. (And, the many other homes we visit throughout the year.)

Today marks the 6th year that, at least to us, Jeffrey J Walker has been quiet. He was the second son of my in-laws. He was not quiet for 36 years. Far from it. He was loud and fun! But, on this morning 6 years ago, he was quiet.

My heart aches with that imagery. I can not fathom the emptiness of that quietness. To lose the "noise" of a child.

Now we know that he is not quiet. We know that he is far more joyful than ever before, and we rejoice with him in that.

But the quiet is unsettling. It's not right.

And I am thankful that God has given us a noisy home. And growing noisier all the time.

Sometimes, the strangest things can be counted as blessings.

The Army Of The Unborn

Nov 16th, 2004

Recently I have been pondering the vast army of people God created *just* for heaven. Many are there by His choice only. They were greatly desired here, but never made it to their parents' arms. Some did, but only for a very short time. We have some friends who only got to spend a few hours with their first baby. So many children of God who did not experience life on this fallen planet.

Millions more are there by *our* choice, and his grace. Abortion has claimed so many lives. But, they go mostly unnoticed since we can somehow overlook the value of lives that we can't really see by calling them a choice.

But I have a new perspective on this.

We have a child who is, we believe, with Jesus as one of the "unborn". And I wonder if God tolerates our incredible insanity where we willingly and purposefully choose to kill our own children, because he is building an army of the unborn. His children (they are, after all, not even really ours…) who never have to experience the hurts of this life. The loneliness. The rejection. The pain. The doubt.

God uses all of those things to sharpen us, to lead us to a deeper trust in him, but they are only part of a fallen world. They will not exist in the new one. In heaven.

So, in a way, I almost feel a strange pride in the fact that one of our family got to be part of that enormous group of people whom God created *just* for heaven.

Awesome.

Just a thought for the day, as we continue to process the events of the past week. I look forward to the day we meet our child, and the countless others God gave the privilege of living at only one address for their entire existence…

Home.

It's Not Fair!

Nov 17th, 2004

For some reason, lots of us expect something out of life. More than something, we expect a lot. There is a whole list of things that we think we deserve. That life somehow owes us.

That, my friends, is faulty thinking.

Life is not fair. I am not even thirty, and I have definitely learned that. At times it gives the appearance that it is fair, but alas, it is only an illusion.

I was watching a special on PBS about the evil empire of Wal*Mart. The show revealed how the company's tactics created such a large retail force that now instead of the manufacturers dictating the cost and volume of a product, the retailers (and the consumers) are now in the driver's seat. That is a role reversal that has caused a chain reaction in a lot of areas, including the loss of manufacturing jobs here in the US.

I do not wish to debate (at this point) the level of humane conditions for workers, or any of the government subsidizing or other props that create the lower cost of business on foreign soil…that may or may not be true. Again, life is not fair. What I want to focus on is the general attitude of the worker who lost his job, and the larger picture of a prevailing attitude of entitlement.

The man who was being interviewed had just lost his job that he had held for about 30 years in a local TV manufacturing plant. Companies like Wal*Mart are purchasing completed products from other countries (rather than importing materials to assemble here) at such a low price that they are making it impossible for companies to compete if they manufacture in the United States. This man was almost whining as he spoke of the woes of his current state of living. No job, no benefits, prospects were bleak of getting another job with the same pay and benefits.

Did you catch that? He didn't think prospects were bleak for another *job*. He didn't think he was going to die of starvation or have to mortgage everything he had just to "make ends meet". He wanted the same pay and benefits. It's not *fair* for Wal*Mart to come in here and take away his life. *"I DON'T WANT TO CHANGE!!!!"*

That's it right there. We are so sure that we are owed whatever list of things we might hold to…a job, a house, a spouse, a family, a child, benefits, a car, *two* cars, high-speed internet (well, now, we *might* be entitled to *that*…). The list goes on and on. Life owes us.

But it doesn't.

"Who of you by worrying can add a single hour to his life?" Jesus asks us. And in another story, God tells a man who was making big plans for his wealth that he's just foolish, cause he was so concerned about that, and he was about to die, and not get any of it.

We *never* know what life is going to bring us. We may lose our job and have to completely change a lifestyle. We may lose our house or a car or everything we own…none of it is permanent. (No matter how much we may convince ourselves otherwise.)

We may lose a child.

Tomorrow is not guaranteed. Nothing is, except the One who never changes. It says that Jesus is the same yesterday, today and forever. [Hebrews 13:8] And it also says that his love will never change (for us) [Romans 8:38-39] and that he will never leave us. [Matthew 28:20]

Life is not fair. It's not "fair" that we lost our baby. It's not fair that the health insurance people didn't want to cover us (though that did work out nicely on our behalf). It's not fair when people lose their jobs and have to start over again. Life is just not fair.

But we are loved. And He is God.

Knowing that makes life a lot better.

SECTION 5

Learning To Trust

Do we really trust him?

January 14th, 2004

You may know the story of Jacob and Esau. Jacob (later known as "Israel") was the trickster, fooling his older and not-so-sharp brother out of his birthright, and his father's blessings—two incredibly important things in those days. Esau was the tough-guy, though, the jock of the family, so when he was murderously angry at his brother, Jacob left town and went to live with his Uncle and cousins. (He ended up marrying BOTH of his cousins...that's a little different than we would do it today...) :-)

Well, God tells Jacob to go back home. This is many years, even decades later. Jacob has amassed quite a wealth of everything you can imagine, including a very large family. God has blessed him. Over, and over, and over again. So, Jacob obeys and heads for his homeland.

On the way, as he wonders what Esau will do, he finds that Esau and 400 of his men are on their way to meet him!!! That sends quite a shock through him. That night he prays a sentence that stands out to me. "O Lord, you told me to return to my land and to my relatives, and *you promised* to treat me kindly." (emphasis mine)

You *promised!*

Those are words that a little child might say when they feel they are being—or even may potentially be—mistreated. Jacob is pretty sure that things don't look like God is going to keep his promise, and that bothers him. In his prayer, he doesn't really show any kind of confidence in God...almost just whining.

Then he proceeds to put together elaborate gifts of EVERYTHING he owns, sending those ahead of the main caravan of people and things. As Esau is met by each group of gifts, he is a bit perplexed. But Jacob keeps sending them, hoping to somehow assuage his anger. (At the time Jacob first left, Esau was letting everyone around him know that he would soon murder his brother...)

You know what happened? For all his effort? For all the huge, elaborate attempts to win his brother's favor? You know where that got him?

God had already done it! Esau was not swayed by any of the presents showered upon him. It wasn't for any of Jacob's efforts, but rather, God had made it happen...*just as He had promised him.*

Don't we do that? Don't we try with all our might to take care of ourselves? When all we have to do is trust God? Jacob even said it in his prayer, but I don't think he really meant it. He said, "You promised to treat me kindly." Apparently he had heard from God that not only should he return, but that all would be well when he arrived. But instead of confidently going forward in what God had told him, Jacob wasted lots of energy trying to earn his own way.

All this just makes me wonder...where am I wasting energy? Where am I not *really* believing God? How can I rest more in Him and wait to see what He has promised me come true? How about you? Where are you being like Jacob and trying to clean up your own messes? Trying to make your own way?

Next time you are following God's lead, don't be like Jacob and try to take matters into your own hands. (Or, remember Peter? Who got to experience walking on TOP of water, in a moment of pure trust, until he too thought he best get this situation under control...) Believe God. For real. That he will really do what He has promised for you.

Life is better when we do.

Trust Me

Jan 3rd, 2005

"Just trust me!"

A phrase that is usually first met with *more* skepticism than was initially present in the truster. When you hear the phrase, "Just *trust* me", it usually makes you wonder if you should. We are, by nature, not trusting.

It certainly feels like we have a tighter grasp on what is best for us than anyone else could. How could we trust the advice of someone else when it goes against what we would do? Why would we allow our power of choice-making to fall into the hands of anyone else?

Because we trust them.

Sometimes, other people know things we don't. Especially the more seasoned among us. It is not universally true of everyone who has more time under their belt, but in general, the more experience in life, the more wisdom. And sometimes, the wisdom from another does not fit snugly with the choice we are about to make, or would like to make.

Whether in the form of a warning, or an admonition, or any sort of advice given, we tend to be skeptical of words of wisdom from people other than ourselves.

Is that natural? Is that normal? In a way. We should be skeptical of Joe Blow on the street who offers his two cents. No matter how wise it may sound, there is no reason for you to believe him. We should be skeptical of Joe Preacher on the TV who offers us his advice. No matter how sweet it may sound, there is no relationship to back it up.

Therein lies the key.

Trust comes only from relationship. The closer the relationship, the tighter the bond, the deeper and freer the trust. I can not think of a relationship where I implicitly trust, no questions asked, and that is an indication that everyone in my life has somehow "lost" my trust along the way. OR, that I still think that I am all-knowing.

All of us are fallible, so the first part is certainly true, however I do believe that a majority of the blame for my mistrust of others falls on my shoulders. I do not trust others because I still think I know best.

In the garden of Eden, Eve sinned, and Adam sinned, not because they were evil people, but at the root, they sinned because they did not trust God. They were egged on by the snake…but ultimately, they ate the fruit God asked them not to because they did not trust him. He didn't really mean not to…It couldn't really be that bad…Maybe He's just trying to keep us down! I won't die…

But they did. And we did. And we will.

All because they could not trust Him. And we continue that heritage every day. Every sin is rooted in our level of trust of our Father. Whether it is a big, bold breakage of one of the heralded Ten Commandments, or something undetectable to the rest of the world. Our level of trust determines our behavior.

The cool thing is, as damning as that sounds, the ultimate culpability is not on us. The blame was placed squarely—and voluntarily—on Jesus' shoulders.

God made him who had no sin to be sin for us so that we might become his righteousness. (2 Corinthians 5:21)

We have the opportunity to become, to *be* the righteousness of God. That is not something we can attain, but rather something given to us. And in 1 Peter, we're told that, "As we know Jesus better, his divine power has given us everything we need for living a godly life." HIS divine power. Sinlessness is not something we can attain, but something he has given to us.

That is not an unknowable thing. I believe that sin is directly related to our level of trust in him. That means the more I trust my Father, the less I will sin. So do I just decide to trust? No. That's not what trust is. Trust is developed over time, through relationship. *As we know Jesus better…*Perhaps that is what Peter was talking about? Perhaps all of life hinges on this? On knowing Jesus?

"And this is the way to have eternal life: to know you the one true God, and Jesus Christ whom you have sent." (John 17:3)

Jesus seemed to think that was pretty important. Relationship is the key. The more we know him, the more we trust him, the less we sin, the more we trust him, the more we know him, etc, etc, etc.

Repentance from sin is definitely our choice. But thankfully, the responsibility to clean up our act does not ultimately rest on us. God is the one who makes us clean. Righteousness comes from him. All we need to do is get to know him better, and the righteousness that is visible to others (and to us) will follow in direct proportion to our trust. Perhaps even greater proportion!

Life is better when we live it with our Father, our Creator, our friend. There is no better way. Everything else falls short.

Trust me.

Responsibility

June 3rd, 2004

So, the other day, in between being mad, I had to laugh at myself. :-)

You may or may not know that through the past several months, God has already taken me to a place that is crazier than most people I know would like to be. That every week, every day, we are not really sure where the money to pay our bills is going to come from. We wake up, we do the day, not knowing what God has in store.

Well, over the past week and a half or so, I have consistently been more and more tense about our financial situation. When I take a step back, I see that really, nothing has changed. But, for some reason, I am noticing the tightness again. There are credit problems I need to fix (not our fault) and an error with a credit card company (this one was more our fault) and well, that whole lack of income thing…it's just been building up.

So do you know what I do???

WRONG!!! I *SHOULD* remember that we have been here before and God always comes through so I should *trust* Him. But I don't.

There is this cycle, that today became more amazing to me than ever before. You see, life has been grand in the past 4 weeks or so. God has shown me cool stuff about me that I needed to know, and cool stuff about Him that I needed to know, and given me a direction to go from there. And I did. And life has been grand.

But you know what often happens when life is grand, when things go our way? We *like* it. We really like it. So much so that we hold on with all of our might to it.

That is what I have been doing. In my desire to be a "good steward" of what God has given me (my family, my time, my resources) I have begun to "manage" too much. Taking too much "responsibility" where in fact I am not actually responsible.

Now I can hear my Dads out there (my Dad and my Dad-in-law) saying, "Nowwwww, wait just a minute there, boy! God wants us to be responsible! He has given us a brain and a body to work hard and to earn a living for our families. What kind of man would not work hard to provide for his family???" And there I think we have a generational terminology gap. See, I think that my generation is more OK with saying we need to give God more room—take on less responsibility—because it means something different to us.

I am so honored that God would trust me with the lives of Jen and our three kiddos. But I know that in the end, I have no control over the money that comes in or the provisions He provides. See, God has put me in this position to lead, but I am only as good at leading as I am at following Him. And in days recent past, I have not been good at that.

And I feel that I am physically, spiritually, emotionally trying too hard. I am feeling too much burden. I am straining to do it all myself, and keep my temporarily happy little world that God has blessed me with the past couple weeks.

"Come to me you who are weary, and I will give you rest. Lay your burdens down"—paraphrase from Matthew 11:28.

God wants us to let Him lead. Do not be lazy—don't shirk honest, hard work. But don't bear the burden. God is our provider. He wants us to know that, and trust that. Don't worry about tomorrow, because today has enough trouble of its own! (another cool quote from Jesus)

I have tried hard today to give up my fight to keep control in my life. It has worked a bit. I have been far less stressed. I have a good test coming up this weekend. There are *so* many things I need to do *right now* it seems. But there is a home school convention about a one-hour drive from our house. A convention which my wife is quite excited about. A convention which we will be attending all day tomorrow and Saturday (with a concert in the middle, back here at home tomorrow night!!) And in the middle of that, our niece is graduating there on Saturday with a party near home on Sunday following a big morning at our church.

So I have a lot of chances to trust God with my time (I won't have any) and my finances (we won't make any) and my family (I sure do love them) :-)

All that to say…what are you holding on to?

Don't You Remember?

June 18th, 2004

I love reading the Bible. It's actually rather entertaining. It's history. I like history. But it's history that unlike my high school textbooks, does not eliminate God from the picture. It puts him in his rightful place as Director of history. I also find that in a way, reading about the crazy kings and all the people who just couldn't get it right, helps me to feel like at least I am doing better than them! Until Asa...

Asa "did what was right in the LORD's sight" as opposed to the other dudes. While they were setting up idols to be worshipped and thumbing their noses at God, he was tearing down the altars and idols and sending out missionaries to re-teach the people the Law of the Lord (the stuff God had given them through Moses hundreds of years earlier.) I identified with this guy, because for the most part, I "do what's right in the LORD's sight." But, there came a crucial juncture in Asa's life that I all too easily also identified with.

"In the thirty-sixth year of Asa's reign, King Baasha of Israel invaded Judah and fortified Ramah in order to prevent anyone from entering or leaving King Asa's territory in Judah. Asa responded by taking the silver and gold from the treasuries of the LORD's Temple and from the royal palace. He sent it to King Ben-hadad of Aram, who was ruling in Damascus, along with this message:

'Let us renew the treaty that existed between your father and my father. See, I am sending you a gift of silver and gold. Break your treaty with King Baasha of Israel so that he will leave me alone.'

Ben-hadad agreed to King Asa's request and sent his armies to attack Israel. They conquered the towns of Ijon, Dan, Abel-beth-maacah, and all the store cities in Naphtali. As soon as Baasha of Israel heard what was happening, he abandoned his project of fortifying Ramah. Then King Asa called out all the men of Judah to carry away the building stones and timbers that Baasha had been using to fortify Ramah. Asa used these materials to fortify the towns of Geba and Mizpah." (2 Chronicles 16:1-6)

That all seems good, eh? The King had a good plan, put it into action, and it *worked!* But, read what happened next…

"At that time Hanani the seer came to King Asa and told him, 'Because you have put your trust in the king of Aram instead of in the LORD your God, you missed your chance to destroy the army of the king of Aram. **Don't you remember** *what happened to the Ethiopians and Libyans and their vast army, with all of their chariots and horsemen? At that time you relied on the LORD, and he handed them all over to you. The eyes of the LORD search the whole earth in order to strengthen those whose hearts are fully committed to him. What a fool you have been! From now on, you will be at war.' Asa became so angry with Hanani for saying this that he threw him into prison. At that time, Asa also began to oppress some of his people." (2 Chronicles 16:7-10)*

Do you see what happened? Unfortunately, I do. Too clearly. Too closely. I have been struggling recently with many things. Money has been super tight, and it has been burdening me a lot more than ever before. I have been trying my hardest to make sure that I pay the bills, and make sure that I take care of my family. I have a friend who is making unwise choices in life that are going to hurt him and a lot of other people. I love him, and care about him and so my heart is deeply burdened by what he is doing and what I need to do to help. I have some sizable debt from various (mostly) business expenses over the past 5 years or so that we continue to try to pay down. But now interest is making that slightly harder to do, so I am burdened by the responsibility of paying off my debt.

Did you notice what happened in that paragraph? That is an accurate description of what is going on in my head right now. Did you see all the "I"s and the "my"s and the "me"s? **DON'T YOU REMEMBER?** Those were the words that stuck out to me as I read this morning. God has done the most amazing things in our life—when we were letting him.

Later in 2 Chronicles 16 it talks about a foot disease that Asa had contracted and it says "even when the disease had gotten life threatening, he did not seek the LORD's help but sought help only from his physicians." That gets me. That makes me think…why don't I remember what *GOD* can do?

I sign autographs. Mostly kids. But I do. And when I do, I make sure to write "Eph 3:20-21" near my name. Because I want people to read that. I want people to know that God can do immeasurably more than we can ask or imagine. That's incredible. That means no matter how big you think God is, he's bigger. Which means he's bigger than anything you're dealing with. But what do we do? *WE* shoulder the burden. *WE* come up with the solutions. *WE* carry out our plans. WE, I, ME, MY.

Don't you remember, Greg, how God provided for you in the past? Don't you remember that your heart was lighter when you trusted *HIM* instead of your own sweat and long hours to provide for your family. Don't you remember that *HE* is the one who changes hearts? Don't you remember that you don't have to do this life on your own?

Don't you remember?

I think I do. :-)

Contentment

July 31st, 2004

We were noticing the other day that there are many people who are not content in life. Most everything that comes from their mouth is negative, or just sad. Many of the politicians are this way, and those who comment on things political (talk show hosts and whatnot). Even many folks we know. Even many Christians (who are the one group of people in the world who should have *NOTHING* to complain about, because we have hope in Jesus that supersedes all the bad stuff here.)

And we just found ourselves wishing we could help somehow. That we could somehow infuse all those folks with even the tiniest bit of the optimism and hope that we have most every day. (I say most every day, because obviously, we are human, and it is obviously hard to have a joy-filled heart everyday.)

But what a world this would be if there were no complaining—if we never even thought to compare ourselves to others, or others to our ideals for them. Or if we could be content with the things that God has given us instead of complaining and pining for more or different. If we could just live every moment as though that were the greatest gift we'd ever been given, and relish the fullness of life in God at *that* moment.

That would be better.

The Bible says these things to us:

1 Thessalonians 5:16-18

Be joyful always; pray continually; give thanks in all circumstances, for this is God's will for you in Christ Jesus.

Colossians 3:12-15

Therefore, as God's chosen people, holy and dearly loved, clothe yourselves with compassion, kindness, humility, gentleness and patience. Bear with each other and forgive whatever grievances you may have against one another. Forgive as the Lord forgave you. And over all these virtues put on love, which binds them all together in perfect unity. Let the peace of Christ rule in your hearts, since as members of one body you were called to peace. And be thankful.

1 Thessalonians 5:11

Therefore encourage one another and build each other up, just as in fact you are doing.

God please help us to see the good that is around us and let you take care of the injustice, and only to speak words that build up and encourage and to be hopeful and patient in You. You are sufficient. More than enough for all that we need. Help us find rest in *You.*

Who Initiates Faith?

Sep 12th, 2004

You hear people talk about God giving them faith to do something, and perhaps you think…that's silly! Faith comes from *ME*, not from God. He gives me something to have faith *IN*, but not the faith.

Well, I would agree with that. But I would add that perhaps there is some truth in the second part of that. "He gives me something to believe in…"

Do you remember the story of Elijah and the prophets of Baal? Israel was deep into idol worship, and ignoring the True God who loved them. Elijah was given the task by God of reminding them many times over just how badly they were choosing. On one occasion he challenged all of the prophets of Baal to take him on in a god-vs-GOD match-up. They accepted.

The story itself is hilarious! There is trash talk and taunting from Elijah, and just plain silliness on the part of the bad-guy prophets. They dance, and yell, and cut themselves trying to get their god to show his goods. But since he is, in fact, IMAGINARY…they get no where.

Then Elijah steps in, and sets the stage for the impossible (you can read 1 Kings 18 for the rest of the story) and then he says this:

1 Kings 18:36

At the time of sacrifice, the prophet Elijah stepped forward and prayed: "O LORD, God of Abraham, Isaac and Israel, let it be known today that you are God in Israel and that I am your servant and have done all these things <u>at your command</u>.

The words underlined were the ones that struck me as I read it. At your command. I had always imagined that this was a clever scheme Elijah had dreamed up. We don't have any account of how God had instructed Elijah to do this, but we do have this line. "[I] have done all these things at your command." I think that is so key to the way that God works.

God does not expect us to come up with the miracles, and ask him for them. It seems to me that God's pattern is to initiate our faith with a leading to believe him for something that is unbelievable.

We see it here with Elijah. He asks God to prove that everything he was doing was not just possible, but actually AT GOD'S COMMAND. *God* initiated this whole "stunt" to show his greatness. Elijah was not making God perform, he was proceeding under the assumption that in fact God *would* perform, since apparently, God said he would.

I did not just decide that God was going to give us the water shoe (see **The Water Shoe**). God put the strong leading in my heart and in my head that he wanted to do something. And He did.

Noah did not decide to build the ark. Moses did not decide to go to Pharaoh and wave a wand and make all those plagues appear and disappear.

God is the initiator. He prompts us when he wants us to trust him for something.

We actually do this with our finances as well. We do not ever ask for money for any music performance. I felt strongly that God wanted me to do this when we started, and he has continued to provide crazily in that way. It wasn't my idea. I want to ask for money quite often, but God reminds me gently that he has a better plan in mind.

And so I believe.

It is my own faith, but it is instigated by a loving Father who knows how He wants to reveal himself to me, and through me.

And boy does he!

So, the more you walk with him, the more you will hear him. And the crazier the thing he asks you to do…do it! And I am pretty sure you will find that crazy following will lead to crazy rewards.

Today

Nov 2nd, 2004

"Give your entire attention to what God is doing right now, and don't get worked up about what may or may not happen tomorrow. God will help you deal with whatever hard things come up when the time comes."—Matthew 6:34 (MSG)

Over the last several years, God has brought that truth very close to home for us. Those are Jesus' words right after the famous ones, "But seek first his kingdom and his righteousness and all these things will be given to you as well." The above quote is from The Message, but I always liked the NIV translation, "Today has enough trouble of its own."

Very realistic. Jesus is not all flowers and balloons and halos.

Jesus' point was not really to wow the crowd with his quite witty sarcasm. He was trying to make the point that no matter how much we fret about tomorrow, and no matter how much we plan and prepare, tomorrow's still gonna come, and today is what we should be focusing on.

The well-known line of Jesus' prayer says "Give us today our *daily* bread". And he meant it. God tried to teach Israel that lesson when they were wandering through the desert for 40 years too. "Just concentrate on today," he said. "Take what you need for you today. Not more. Trust me for tomorrow. *Today* you will have what you need, and *I* will take care of you *today*."

I think that's the part God wants to teach all of us.

He is going to take care of us. *He* is going to give us what we need today.

I have really been struggling with that on this trip. Money of course plays a big part in all of the stuff God seems to want to teach us, not because we struggle with materialism or greed or anything with money really, but simply because we really constantly have just what we need for today. Not enough for tomorrow…until it's today.

Well, we have this new Christmas CD. And it's been selling fairly well. Which is good. But not quite as well as I'd hoped. So I continue to try and scheme and look ahead and use everything at my disposal to bring in more money so we don't have to wonder about tomorrow. I want to try to ensure that we will have enough money for today AND tomorrow. When will I learn????????

How can I so constantly forget? God has shown me so often that it doesn't matter how much I scheme for tomorrow, it only frustrates me. Whether I am frustrated, exhausted, worried, or completely at peace and trusting him, he still provides what I need today. Everyday.

But I think I am hinging all my hope on a big craft show we get to sing at in December. I have been led to believe that this 2-day event for 60,000 people will be quite lucrative for us in CD sales. So, I am optimistic that we will sell as much as has been predicted (which would pay off most or even ALL of our significant debt, which would be awesome).

But many things along this trip keep putting that weekend in jeopardy. Snow for one. Jen's health for another. The baby is making her really extra tired. Money for another. If you were one to look ahead to tomorrow, you might think we would not have enough money to make it home (or even to the next gig?)

But I am not. I choose not to be. Really.

My hope is not in a gig. My hope is not in my best plans and schemes. My hope is in my Father who loves me.

He will take care of me today. And I will not ruin today by worrying about tomorrow.

God helps us be thankful for the day he has given us today. With all its promise, and with all its trouble.

He will get us through.

Till Tomorrow becomes Today.

Today—Part II

Nov 7th, 2004

Do you remember a few days back, God was teaching me to live for Today. Not to be worrying about tomorrow, but to know that He will take care of us today?

We left the house with only the $6 cash that our host friends gave us to get a little dinner after our show. They were watching our kids, which was worth 700x the $6 they donated to our stomach fund. We had no other cash, and for all intents and purposes, nothing in our bank accounts.

But, we had joy. Really, we did. We were not worried about what is next, not worried about our bills, or our food, or our kids. We both really knew God was going to take care of that.

We sang for about 10 people total. Mostly it was 3 nice old ladies. (And the store owner/sound guy along with another musician who sang that night). The music was well received, and as I sang it, my heart was lifted as I remembered the truth of what I sang—life really is all about being a child of God. Trusting him, spending the days with him, loving him, being loved by him…everything else then falls into place.

Including money.

After everything was over, the store owner pulled me aside, and said he wanted to give us a check, but he needed to go home to do it, so he asked if we could wait around a bit. He also mentioned he wanted to give us a *thousand dollars*.

Dude.

I just can't even explain to you how this feels, even as I type this a day later. That someone we don't even know would be so amazingly generous to us is beyond comprehension.

God provides yet again. In a spectacular way. At just the right time. Using his people to both give and be given to.

Whoa.

Dude.

Amazing.

Unreal.
Cool. :-)

Love = Trust

Nov 21st, 2004

We listened today to a major portion of an audio book received last week from our friends in Elk Grove. It is by a man named Wayne Jacobsen, who has a really cool view on life in the Kingdom. I believe you can get all his books at Amazon.com, or check his blog page at www.lifestream.org.

Something he said in Chapter 5 of this book really caught my ear tonight, and I wanted to share it with you before I went to bed.

"You'll trust Him only to the degree that you are certain of His love for you."

That is *so true*. The root of our faith, of our trust in our Father is understanding how high and deep and long and wide is the love of Jesus for us. He loves us not based on what we do for him, or if we continue in that, but only because we are his. He made us, and wants so badly to have a relationship with us, that he gave his life to prove it.

When we let that sink in, we can really begin to trust him. If God had lots of requirements on us before we can hang out with him, or even before he was hung on a cross to die, it would be a bit harder to trust him. If he was a big, scary, unpredictably vengeful God...he'd be harder to trust.

But Paul said we have been given a spirit by which we call him Abba, Father. And Jesus compared us to God's children, whom He loves to please.

It's not all about life on easy street for us. It is all about life in the full assurance that we are accepted and loved by our Creator, who thought we were worth suffering an agonizing death on a cross.

Once we are confident in his love, we can *really* trust him. When we really trust him, we see him work in our lives and we love him more. Which leads to deeper trust...which leads to more relationship, which leads to more love...

You get the point.

Innocence

Dec 15th, 2004

We really do have to learn to be bad.

There are times when I know that statement above is *not* true…I see the evidence of selfish, sinful, mistrust of their father in all of my kids from nearly their first day of life.

But today with a crowd of kids from 1st through 8th grade, I remembered again, skepticism is learned. Bad habits are learned. Mistrust of our Father is learned. Selfishness is bred by a constant barrage of self-esteem bashing from within and without. We must fight to get what is ours, because we can't trust anyone else to do it or get it for us…not even Father.

We were explaining the Christmas story to the kids again this morning, and they knew it completely. And my point with adults is that the essence of the story is missed. The pure and insane love that God has for us, and the sheer joy He finds in just *loving* us is profoundly astonishing. No one should love me like that. I have convinced myself (or have been convinced) of my many faults, and know that I am certainly not worth anyone's life…especially the life of the Life Giver!

But I am. And they are. And the kids already know it.

They have not yet known the emptiness of failure. The loneliness of rejection. The pain of being different or undesirable. At some point, they will experience those things. We are all very good at pointing out the shortcomings in other people, either directly or inferred.

But God does not. His love is so complete and so penetrating to our core, that no shortcoming or failure or handicap or anything at all really could keep his love from us. Or, keep him from loving us. We let the world and ourselves convince us that we are not worth loving, but we are.

Jesus said we should become like little children. *Then* we will see the Kingdom of heaven. There is purity. There is trust. There is innocence.

That is what we should strive for. To trust him more. To understand the depth of his love and live in the freedom of that. There is where our life is. There is hope. There is peace.

There…is Christmas.

The Water Shoe

October 29th & 30th, 2003

This collection of articles was written "real-time", not after the fact (until the fact had actually happened) and so we wanted to present them that way, but we have put them together in one chapter calling it *The Water Shoe*. We still have the water shoe. It only cost us a few dollars at a Wal-Mart somewhere along the way, but it is now priceless for what—for Who—it represents. So, sit back and read the story of the day we found *The Water Shoe*...

Flowery Prayers

October 29th, 2003

I was humbled again. By my son Ian. I love it when he does that. Really.

We were praying, and sometimes Ian is a bit embarrassed to talk with God in front of people, even Mom and Dad. Tonight he was again, but He decided to.

A bit of background...

We went to the beach tonight after sunset (yes, the water was still quite warm!) and Ian and I were having a bunch of fun jumping waves. On one jump, over a large wave, Ian returned to the ground quite upset, and I finally got out of him that he lost his water shoe!!! I spent 10 minutes feeling around for it, and looking around in the moonlit water. No luck. And all I could think about was the trust of Ian for his Dad to find his shoe (that seemed to me to be quite precious to him) and how I could not do it. So I kept thinking that God is in control of oceans. And I kept asking him to help me find it, wash it up on shore, or put it in my hand. Whatever he wanted to do for my son Ian who completely trusts both of his Dads. Well, no shoe, but I kept thinking that we should just come back tomorrow morning...so, I went back to Ian and told him that. And we are going to go back and look for it tomorrow morning.

So, fast forward to tonight, praying before Ian goes to bed. And Ian decides he can pray without getting embarrassed. He simply asked God to "please put the shoe on the beach so we can find it tomorrow. Thanks." That was so cool.

The part that humbled me was not that. We continued to pray, and this time I was praying for our friend Kayla who is sick in the hospital with pneumonia. I thanked God for being big and powerful and asked him to help in many ways to heal Kayla, and to help Kayla's Mom have peace as she trusts Him.

Simple. Plain English. That's how I would talk to my dad, so that's how I talk to my Dad.

But Ian wanted to pray for Kayla, too. So he did.

"God, we know that you are mighty, and powerful…and we ask you to…get the…to…uh…. (many words)…help the doctors get medicine to help Kayla's body to get better. So she doesn't die."

Notice a difference? I did. Ian was getting all flowery (in his best four-year-old way…) because I guess I do. I try hard to just be real with God. Guess I can try even more. I don't want Ian thinking God is a distant, unapproachable God who only listens if we use the right words.

Thanks Ian for a fresh perspective.

Thanks Dad for Ian.

You are both awesome. (In different ways of course…)

Ian's Shoe

October 30th, 2003

Just a quick update on Ian's shoe…

We got up this morning at 7am, which is like 3 hours before Ian usually gets up! We walked right out the door (Dad and Ian) and headed to the beach. We asked God as we walked to show us where He put the shoe…and we started looking. We probably looked for 30 min or so, up and down the beach where we had lost it. No luck. I finally told Ian, "Why don't we go home and we'll come back and see if God wants to give it to us later. Sometimes God likes us to learn to trust Him by waiting."

So we did. We made it back to the beach around 1:30pm or so with the whole family, and started to look again. We were just having fun, too…but Ian really wanted to find his shoe. He said, "Ask God again, Dad!" I told him, "Yeah, I can't do anything about this Ian. If God wants to give you your shoe, He will, if not, then we'll just have to get another one."

Within one minute I think, Ian had gone up to be with Mom (out of the water) and they started walking down the beach, and there were shouts of excitement…THEY FOUND IT!!! It was just sitting right in the beach wash (which Ian and I had checked at least 4 times earlier today).

Wow. Thanks God. You are the Wave Maker. The Oceans (and the Gulfs) obey your commands. And you love your children so much. We are amazed at God's abilities and his love for us.

Hope you know that too.

From My Perspective...

October 30th, 2003

I just wanted to add some more on the fantastic faith story of Ian's water shoe. Just some thoughts from my head throughout the whole thing.

Can God Really Do It?

That thought obviously kept going through my head. In a way. You know, I really had no problem believing that God *could* bring Ian's shoe out of the water and neatly onto the shore for us...but where my mind betrays me or gets me into trouble is on the "does he want to" side of things. I mean, what does God care about a shoe?

But He Cares About Ian...

But I kept coming back to the fact that it's not about the shoe. It's about how much God loves Ian—and even me—in this. He loves it when we come to him believing that he exists and that he rewards those who earnestly seek him. (Hebrews 11:6)

Faith Like A Child.

You know, I actually saw Ian's simple faith waiver a bit. But it wasn't as insecure as my wavering. I wonder if God would ever do something big and God-like for me...but Ian didn't worry about that. He just wondered when it would happen. He *knew* God would do it. That was so cool. I did too actually. It was honestly the most confident I have been in a while, and I just smiled every time I was talking to God cause I really knew He was going to do it.

Moments of Doubt.

There were plenty of moments when I had looked and asked and found nothing where I wanted to just give up. And I would talk to God again and ask Him what should I do...lead me to the shoe. (That rhymed...) I knew that even if God did not come through with the shoe, there would be some awesome story of His provision. I was confident in that.

Celebration!

You know, I honestly thought I would celebrate more. But all I wanted to do was smile and worship God. We sang some, we shouted out "GOD IS AWESOME!" and just had fun. But in the end, we were really expecting Him to do it! We knew he could, and we thought he would. Amazing.

I think that is how God wants us to live. Completely trusting Him, even when it doesn't make sense, or seem possible. There are so many chances we have in life to trust that God is bigger. Sickness being one of them. Our friend's daughter is really, really sick. And they love Jesus. A lot. They are in a crisis of belief. Can God fix this? Will he? Does he love us? They know all the answers, but now they have to trust him.

God gave Ian his shoe back today so he will have a reason to trust Him in the future with bigger stuff. Our friends are dealing with a very tough situation right now, where they have to trust God. God has given them plenty of shoes. That is what they are holding on to, and taking comfort in right now—the shoes God has given them.

What are your shoes? Can you think of one? Or several? God gives us little markers along the way where we see Him very clearly working or leading in our lives. And it's when we look back at those that we can look forward in trust. Faith is being *sure* of what we hope for and *certain* of what we do not see. Without faith it is impossible to please God, because anyone who comes to him must believe that he exists and that he rewards those who earnestly seek him. Words of wisdom from the book of Hebrews.

Faith requires action. God gives us reasons to trust him (shoes) and then something happens where we *have* to trust him. That's when we remember the shoes, and trust that He has another one for us.

Tonight, celebrate Ian's shoe, and remember yours. And thank God for his amazing love and faithfulness. And trust him. Really trust him.

The Journey Continues...

Continue to share the journey at **www.GregsHead.net**

Write to: P.O. Box 36, Palmyra, NY 14522.

For more from Greg's Head visit:
www.gregshead.net

0-595-34635-9

www.ingramcontent.com/pod-product-compliance
Lightning Source LLC
Chambersburg PA
CBHW061300280526
45784CB00002B/839